Paul Schalow
April 9, 1998

BLACK EGGS

Kurihara Sadako with daughter Mariko. 1937. Courtesy of Kurihara Sadako.

BLACK EGGS

Poems by
KURIHARA SADAKO

Translated with an Introduction
and Notes by
RICHARD H. MINEAR

CENTER FOR JAPANESE STUDIES
UNIVERSITY OF MICHIGAN
ANN ARBOR, MICHIGAN
1994

© 1994 **Center for Japanese Studies**

THE UNIVERSITY OF MICHIGAN

108 Lane Hall, Ann Arbor, MI 48109–1290

Michigan Monograph Series in Japanese Studies, Number 12

Library of Congress Cataloging in Publication Data

Kurihara, Sadako. *1913 - 2005*
   [Kuroi tamago. English]
   Black eggs / by Kurihara Sadako ; translated by Richard H. Minear.
      xviii, 329 p. 23.5 cm. — (Michigan monograph series in Japanese studies ;
  no. 12)
   Includes translation of her selected later poems.
   ISBN 0–939512–63–7
   1. Kurihara, Sadako—Translations into English. I. Minear,
Richard H. II. Title. III. Series.
PL855.U66A26 1994
895.6'15—dc20   93–31472
                                               CIP

This book was set in Palatino and Gill Sans
Book design by Judy Stopke
Composed by The Composing Room, Grand Rapids, Michigan
Printed and bound by Thomson-Shore, Inc.

The paper used in this publication meets the requirements of the ANSI Standard
Z39.48–1984 (Permanence of Paper).

In the rubble a single wildflower
sent out small white blossoms.
From the burned soil filled with the bones
of fathers, mothers, brothers, relatives,
from the now-silent ruins
where every living thing burned to death:
a small life that taught us to live.
Hiroshima, carrying on from that day—
a flower blooming in the midst of destruction.

—MARCH 1988

Contents

Tanka

PART TWO: Selected Later Poems

The Poet

Hiroshima

Japan

Preface

JAPAN LOST THE WAR and then, very quickly, became a great economic power. Now it has hurt America's pride by its arrogant pronouncements and by buying up American land, buildings, and culture. Both countries engage in criticizing each other—Japan-bashing, America-bashing—a situation that is cause for concern. But I believe that even though each side bashes the other and even though the two governments wish to be linked in military alliance, the citizens of the two countries are bound firmly together in the cause of peace.

In preparing this translation, Richard Minear has spared no effort to make available to Americans the desire of Japanese citizens for peace. And when I think of the existence—in numbers truly befitting America—of American intellectuals, poets, and writers, my respect for American democracy and my trust in American democracy deepens, and I can only hope for peaceful and friendly relations between Japan and America. When the atomic bomb was dropped on Hiroshima, the poet Herman Hagedorn wrote "The Bomb That Fell on America"; the poem was translated into Japanese in 1950. Because of its length, I will quote only a part.

> Lord, we have not forgotten Pearl Harbor.
> We have not forgotten the peace envoys, stalling Roosevelt and
>   Cordell Hull while the planes were already on the way to
>   drop death on our ships and our men. . . .
> But we know that more than half of those whom the bomb
>   obliterated at Hiroshima were women and children. . . .
> The bomb that fell on Hiroshima fell on America too. . . .

It erased no church, vaporized no public building, reduced no
    man to his atomic elements.
But it fell, it fell. . . .
Who loosed this terror upon mankind?
We know, and the world knows.
It is America, the idealist among the nations. The people with
    the great humanitarian dream . . .
America loosed the bomb that killed a hundred thousand
    people in Hiroshima and shook the foundations of the
    world. . . .

Thus Hagedorn laments America's moral bankruptcy.

But the dropping of the bomb did not happen out of the blue; it was the result of Japan's attack on Asia and the Pacific in the fifteen-year war. What's more, the Allies had issued the Potsdam Proclamation on 26 July 1945 and had given Japan final warning to respond by surrendering unconditionally before 3 August. Even though the war was lost, the Japanese government ignored the Potsdam declaration in the interests of preserving the emperor system. So the dropping of the bomb was both an American act and a Japanese sacrifice in the name of preserving the emperor system.

Let me speak briefly about the Gulf War. Despite hopes and actions for a peaceful resolution, the violent acts of a small country were met with a military force that had America at its center. Destruction and butchery were carried out, and many people were turned into refugees. Former Attorney General Ramsay Clark accused George Bush before the international war crimes tribunal of violating nineteen provisions of international law.

Moreover, Bernard Lown, American president of International Physicians Protesting Nuclear War (IPPNW), conducted an on-the-spot investigation during the Gulf War. He reports that high-tech weapons are inhumane and as destructive as nuclear weapons, and that more than one thousand nuclear weapons were deployed in the Middle East. He published the results of his research on the deterioration of American society since President Reagan's great arms buildup. He argues that the collapse of the Soviet Union is a question not of socialism or capitalism but of the unproductive arms race, and he warns that America too may soon follow in the footsteps of the Soviet Union.

Charles Overby, emeritus professor at Ohio University, has urged the formation of an American Article 9 Society to support and universalize Article 9 of the Japanese Constitution. He suggests that there can be no world peace unless all countries in the world adopt the principle of renouncing war as in Article 9. We take heart because we have gained a million, ten million allies.

I am deeply grateful to the Center for Japanese Studies at the University of Michigan and to Richard Minear for making this volume possible. I hope for growing friendship between Japan and America.

KURIHARA SADAKO
MAY 1992

d. march 6, 2005

Acknowledgments

I FIRST MET KURIHARA SADAKO in 1983 in Hiroshima. I was then translating Ōta Yōko's *City of Corpses* and had gone to Hiroshima to meet Ōta's half-sister, Nakagawa Ichie. That was my first trip to Hiroshima—in my twenty-third year as a Japan scholar. (Like many of my colleagues in the field of Japanese studies, I had been avoiding Hiroshima.) When Nakagawa arrived at our meeting, she was accompanied by Kurihara. I had no idea then who Kurihara was. Now I know. I thank her for her willingness to grant me translation rights to her poetry, for her responsiveness to my inquiries, and for her hospitality in Hiroshima in June 1992.

My second major debt is to Yasuko Fukumi. A poet herself and old enough to remember the war years, Fukumi was the ideal person to help me through the many problems I encountered. She went over each poem with me to explore meaning and tone, she wrote Kurihara a series of letters to inquire about poems that were open to more than one interpretation, and she reacted to several drafts of translation. Her admiration for Kurihara reinforced my own.

My third major debt is to Christopher Drake. Drake served as the outside reader for the Center for Japanese Studies and then went far beyond that role. Though busy with his own research, he took long hours to comment—virtually line by line—on my translations. In short, he was a model critic.

For readings of the manuscript I thank my parents, Gladys and Paul Minear, who have played a similar role in virtually all my writing, Doris Bargen, and Edwin Cranston. For assistance with the Prange Collection, I thank Frank

Joseph Shulman and Hisayo Murakami. For general support I thank Bill and Nancy Doub of *The Bulletin of Concerned Asian Scholars*, which published early versions of nine of these poems and approved their inclusion in this volume, and David Goodman. Bruce Willoughby of the Center for Japanese Studies has been a most accommodating editor.

Needless to say, I am responsible for the final product in all its shortcomings.

RICHARD H. MINEAR
JUNE 1993

Translator's Introduction

KURIHARA SADAKO was born in Hiroshima and was in Hiroshima on 6 August 1945. She has lived in Hiroshima ever since. She is a Hiroshima poet and a poet of the atomic bomb. But her poetry is "atomic bomb literature" only in part. It is also poetry of the Pacific War, of family, of love. And the importance of the atomic bomb to the world since August 1945 makes her poetry universal. As the title of one of her later poems states, "The Future Begins Here"—here being the cenotaph in Peace Park.

Today Kurihara is a leader of the antinuclear movement in Japan. She composes poems, reads her poems, writes essays, and edits "atomic bomb literature." She also acts: in June 1992 she took part in the campaign against sending Japanese troops abroad under the auspices of the United Nations and in a sit-in protesting the words of an American delegate to a United Nations conference in Hiroshima. Indeed, her political activities may keep critics from realizing that Kurihara Sadako is one of postwar Japan's important poets.

There are other reasons for the fact that Kurihara the poet is relatively unknown in Japan today: she is a woman; she writes from strong political convictions; she lives in Hiroshima, not Tokyo; and she publishes her poems and essays in journals that are hardly mainstream. Paradoxically, the same factors may contribute to the strength of her poetry.

Kurihara's Life: Birth to 6 August 1945

Kurihara Sadako was born Doi Sadako in Hiroshima city in 1913, second daughter of a farm family. Except for scattered poems in *Kuroi tamago* [Black Eggs] ("Father, Mother," "New-Soldier Brother" and "First Letter"), she has not written about the family into which she was born.[1]

Kurihara's formal schooling took place between 1919, when she entered primary school, and 1930, when she graduated from a girls' higher school. In terms of the curriculum of today's American schools, her education was perhaps the equivalent of four years of college, but the school itself—run by the prefecture—was hardly an elite institution. Doi Sadako composed her first poems in 1926, when she was thirteen. Her first published poem appeared in Hiroshima's newspaper, *Chūgoku shinbun*, in 1930, when she was seventeen.

At eighteen, Doi Sadako met Kurihara Tadaichi, the man with whom she would spend the next fifty years. Then twenty-five, Tadaichi came from the same village as Sadako, but he had already moved into a larger world. A middle-school drop-out, he had thrown himself into leftist politics after the Great Earthquake of 1923. In Tokyo he took part in anarchist meetings. This activity made him a marked man; when he returned to Hiroshima from Tokyo at the end of the 1920s, he was under police surveillance. The state deemed him a "quasi-incompetent," a legal status it accorded those who strayed over the borders of what was ideologically acceptable. Thus he could offer Sadako no security at all. Far from it: "Our road will be a thorny one. Come along provided you realize that." Kurihara Sadako calls that statement the clincher. Looking back, she has called her decision "reckless," but she has also cited the whole episode as evidence of the idealism and ardor that the world needs: "Youth dreams of tomorrow and creates the future; no matter how old I get, I want to be youthful to the day I die."[2]

The two ran away from Hiroshima, going by boat to Matsuyama on Shikoku. They soon ran out of money, however, and on their return to Hiroshima, the police picked her up and returned her to her family. Though they treated their daughter with kindness, her family would not countenance Tadaichi; her father, in particular, stated that she would never marry "that traitor as long as I am alive." Reacting against close parental supervision, Sadako proposed that she emigrate to Brazil. In her words: "I said I'd go to Brazil because, first, I had some slight hope that what was impossible in Japan might be possible if I went abroad, and, second, I thought I wanted in any case to leave Japan."

Emigration involved being formally adopted into a family that was emigrating, and Kurihara took that step. It also involved going to Kobe for papers and for embarkation (on a ship named the *Buenos Aires*). She stayed in a reception center for those emigrating; her father stayed nearby in a Kobe hotel.

The night before her ship was to sail, she received a telegram: "Meet me at Sannomiya Station at six o'clock. Rinko." Rinko was Ōhara Rinko, a close acquaintance to whom her family could not object (see "Elegy"), but in fact the telegram was from Tadaichi. Sadako and Tadaichi met at Sannomiya Station at six o'clock, and Sadako never did go to Brazil. They lived in Osaka, Tokushima, and Matsuyama before economic hardship drove them back to Hiroshima.[3] Though he was a middle-school drop-out, Tadaichi had never stopped learning. His anarchism found a ready audience in Sadako. She remembers reading Kropotkin, in particular, and one of the lighter poems of *Kuroi tamago* is, indeed, "Letter—to Peter Kropotkin."

Their first child was born in poverty in 1932, when Kurihara was 19; that child, their only son, died of malnutrition in 1934. Daughters followed: Mariko in 1935 and Junko in 1939 (see "The Birth of Junko"). In 1931 Kurihara's parents had cut off relations with her in protest against her marriage to Tadaichi, but relations resumed on the birth of her second daughter in 1939.

Between 1937 and 1944, the Kuriharas ran a kitchen-goods store in Hiroshima. They shared a life on the home front that was never good and soon got worse. She was on call to neighborhood mobilizations: labor details and air-raid drills. (On 5 August 1945, the day before the bomb, she worked clearing firebreaks in Tenjin-chō, close to ground zero.) Despite his legal status, Tadaichi was subject to more serious mobilization.

In July 1940, Tadaichi was called up to serve on a hospital ship and was briefly in the China theater until he contracted beriberi and was sent home in November. His willingness to talk about the Japanese atrocities he had witnessed in Shanghai got him arrested. Here is Kurihara's later account of Tadaichi's arrest:

> Having contracted severe beriberi, my husband was demobilized in November of that year [1940], and for a while he was a patient in Hiroshima Army Hospital. After being discharged from the hospital, he met an acquaintance on the bus, and the acquaintance asked, "I hear you were in Shanghai. Once you saw the battlefields, you must have come to understand the difficulties that beset the soldiers of the Imperial Army. I'll bet you learned that your earlier antiwar thoughts were a youthful error."
>
> My husband replied, "No. When I saw the reality of war, I understood absolutely that war is something that should not be conducted. The sooner we stop it—even one day sooner—the better." And he spoke of what he had seen and heard in Shanghai. In Shanghai he had witnessed a scene in which Japanese soldiers—cheering all the while—plunged their swords into the genitals of the corpse of a woman soldier of the Eighth Route Army who had been killed by machine-gun fire.
>
> The man on the bus reported my husband to the authorities, and the next day he was asked to go voluntarily to the police station . . . and he did so. The following day I went to visit him, taking some toilet articles. . . . Several days later, after the investigation was complete, they let him go, but the documents were forwarded to the prosecutor.[4]

The authorities apparently took no further action.

In 1944 wartime shortages meant no goods to sell, and Tadaichi and Sadako eventually closed the store. Tadaichi was drafted again in 1944, this time to work in the Mitsubishi Precision Instrument factory in Gion, just north of

Hiroshima; in July the family evacuated from the city to Gion, which has remained Kurihara's home ever since. Many of the poems in *Kuroi tamago* describe the wartime conditions; see in particular "War Close Up," "The Fox's Gold Coins," "On a Day of Powdery Snow," "To a Friend, Evacuated," and "Last Effects."

On 6 August 1945 Kurihara was at home, four kilometers from ground zero. "The Day of the Atomic Bomb" speaks of her experience that day with riveting intensity, and many other poems deal with her experience of the aftermath of the bomb.

Kurihara's Life: 6 August 1945 to the Present

After the war Kurihara Sadako involved herself in literary and political activities. Indeed, the Kuriharas' planning for the postwar cultural scene began even before the defeat. The first fruit of their efforts was the publication (in March 1946) of *Chūgoku bunka*, a special, first issue on the atomic bomb, which marked the rebirth of literary activity in Hiroshima. It was in planning this issue that Kurihara first met Hosoda Tamiki, a leftist writer who had lived in Tokyo and had returned to Hiroshima in May. In 1946 he wrote a preface for *Kuroi tamago*, and in it he speaks of his initial impression of the Kuriharas: "The Kuriharas could talk well of many topics: politics, society, ideas. I was a bit surprised to find such a couple—it is perhaps impolite to say so—in the provinces."[5]

Kurihara Tadaichi spent his life in political, not literary, activity, but occasionally he did write. He wrote "Peace and Socialism" for the August 1946 issue of *Chūgoku bunka*, the journal on which he and Sadako worked together.[6] In that essay Tadaichi speaks of the horror of the atomic bomb but draws from that very horror a message of optimism. He begins:

> Paradoxically, by the severity of its very own destructive
> power the atomic bomb—quintessence of science—has unified

the opinions of all humankind in favor of an end to the age of wars.

Japan received the baptism of the first atomic bomb, and it has disarmed completely, stated expressly in its constitution its renunciation of war, and set out on the road to a new human ideal. Those once great heroes who adorned themselves with gold braid and stars and decorated their chests with sashes and hung long swords at their waists, who bestrode the systematic class system of the military—they now appear in the court-room of the Tokyo trial, mere crazed psychotics.

Think of the long era of war that these few psychotics brought about.

Tadaichi writes of the mobilization of the intellectuals:

> newspapers, magazines, writers, poets, scholars, calligraphers. Thus the nation at war, having won over the pillars of society's conscience, caused the ignorant masses to dig up pine roots [for making ersatz aviation fuel], and to arm themselves with bamboo spears. . . . Impossible things, ridiculous if measured by common sense, were carried out "for victory" and consid-ered reasonable.

Scholars left the university to die in battle; socialists flocked to the cause, lending it respectability. Expatriate activists who worked against the war were denounced as unpatriotic and treasonous sell-outs, but "in a nation-state with a low cultural level," state good is not compatible with higher causes. If such people achieve their goals of raising the cul-tural level of the state, then "some day state good and world good may be one and the same."

Tadaichi continues: "In a time when the doctrine of a truth that transcends state boundaries, a love that tran-scends state boundaries, was bedecked in malice, only the socialists, and they alone, resisted the war actively and pas-sively." He cites Romain Rolland's *Above the Battle* (1915), in which the French pacifist compares the sycophantic intellec-tuals of Kaiser Wilhelm's Imperial Germany with the dis-affected intellectuals (Tadaichi mentions Kropotkin, Tolstoi, Dostoevsky, and Gorki) of Tsarist Russia: "on this point Ja-pan's artists and scholars were just like Germany's; by be-coming friends of the state, they became enemies of truth."

Tadaichi describes the patriotic fervor with which mothers raised children and wives sent husbands off to war, and he stresses the dangers of such fanaticism:

> In such a situation nothing can serve as a brake on war—not truth, not the maternal love of women, not love of God, not socialism. But paradoxically, the fearsome power of the atomic bomb, born to further the purposes of war, now demands that the world renounce war.

He mentions Malthus and Darwin and "the market and the competition for resources that are the true cause of war . . . [I]f the world is reorganized with new wisdom, these of course will disappear."

The world has grown smaller, cooperation has become more fruitful than competition, and "the day of a single great world federation" is no longer merely a dream: "State particularism is headed inevitably toward internationalism." So humankind faces a bright future—unless it reverts to war once more. But the world after a nuclear holocaust would be of little use to the few survivors. Tadaichi concludes: "We who were born like the phoenix from the flames of the atomic bomb must pay for world peace with our bodies. That can happen only if the cold hard fact of defeat is engraved onto Japan's heart, and Japan itself undertakes uncompromisingly to reform itself." What comes through most clearly in this essay—Tadaichi wrote it less than a year after a serious bout with radiation sickness—is a firmness of will and an indomitable optimism.

Kurihara Tadaichi ran for political office and was elected to Hiroshima's prefectural assembly in 1955. He served three terms (twelve years); elected as an independent, he joined the Socialist Party. Kurihara Sadako played an important role in many of Tadaichi's political activities. She also became involved increasingly in issues of broader—national and international—political import. She wrote poems in support of the movement against the U.S.-Japan Security Treaty (1960), poems attacking U.S. policy in Vietnam, and poems attacking nuclear power in Japan and around the world (Three Mile Island, Chernobyl). She took on Japanese politicians of the conservative mainstream, from the mayor of Hiroshima to prime ministers to the emperor; she fought against the resurgence of nationalism and the Japanese flag.

The major early survivor-writers of Hiroshima's atomic experience died much too early: Hara Tamiki, by suicide, in 1951; Tōge Sankichi in 1953; Ōta Yōko in 1963; and Shōda Shinoe in 1965. That left Kurihara Sadako and a few others such as the poet Ōhara Miyao (1905–92) and the critic Nagaoka Hiroyoshi. On Nagaoka's death in 1989, Kurihara wrote a poem comparing herself with Nagaoka and Hara, both made, she suggests, of finer stuff than she:

> I, made of coarser stuff—
> I didn't fall from the sky;
> I don't rise up into the sky.
> I have to crawl along the ground.
> And I have to see
> what those who could not bear to live
> could not bear to see.[7]

We may wish to differ with Kurihara as to the stuff of which she is made. For almost fifty years she has continued to "see/ what those who could not bear to live/ could not bear to see." Thirty-two years old when the bomb fell, she will be eighty-two when, in 1995, we commemorate 6 August 1945 for the fiftieth time.

Particularly after 1965, she stressed the Japanese role as victimizer in the Pacific War. The poem for which she is most famous today outside of Japan, "When We Say 'Hiroshima'" (May 1972), speaks eloquently on the score of Japan as victimizer. It is perhaps symbolic of the Japanese scene until very recently that Kurihara is known in Japan most widely not for this poem but for "Let Us Be Midwives!" from *Kuroi tamago*.

Kurihara's political engagement included reaching out to the international peace community in prose and poetry, defending atomic bomb literature and its writers against hostile critics, and drawing parallels between atomic bomb literature and the literature of the European holocaust. Political engagement also meant choices that left Kurihara at odds with former allies. For example, in 1961 the Soviet Union resumed nuclear testing. Japanese antinuclear groups, overwhelmingly leftist in orientation, had to decide whether to indict the Soviet Union in the same terms that they had used for the United States. Kurihara was a member of a group of women artists and decided to attack all nuclear testing. As Kurihara wrote in an essay of 1980: "Contamination of the environment and damage to the human body are the same no matter whether the country exploding the bomb is capitalist or socialist."[8] That decision left her an outcast. She turned that experience into the poem, "The Crow."

Tadaichi died on 15 October 1980. Despite the difficulties that marked relations between them, difficulties that Kurihara writes about in many of her poems (see "Rivalry," "Love," "Passion," "The Vow," and "Record of My Passion" in *Kuroi tamago*, and "Words Died" in the section The Poet in her later poems), the two did not separate, and on Tadaichi's death in 1980, Kurihara wrote "In Memoriam."

In *Off Center*, Masao Miyoshi discusses the self-restraint that characterized Japan's public life during the Shōwa emperor's final illness. He reports:

> The extent of the restraint was startling: loud music, drinking parties, neon advertisements, foreign travel, festivities, or any other highly visible events were restricted or canceled. Most entertainment performances were allowed to continue, presumably as long as they were contained within a definite and inconspicuous site. There were no explicit rules of conduct because—and this is a little unsettling—people tacitly understood what to do and what not to do.[9]

Kurihara was not about to comply; instead, she organized an anthology of dissenting poems about the emperor, including her own vitriolic "The Day the Shōwa Era Ends." (In June 1989 she extended her criticism of Hirohito to his successor Akihito. She considered the Shinto ceremony accompanying his enthronement as a contradiction of the postwar constitution and "absolutely unacceptable."[10]) Nor—though she had used pen names earlier in her career—did she seek anonymity now. The attempted assassination of Mayor

Motoshima of Nagasaki on 18 January 1990 focussed attention on the activities of right-wing hoodlums. In 1991 Kurihara too received telephoned threats, but she was not to be intimidated.[11]

In 1990 Kurihara was awarded the third Tanimoto Kiyoshi Prize. (Tanimoto was the Methodist minister who figures so prominently in John Hersey's *Hiroshima*; the first recipient of the Tanimoto Prize was the late American journalist Norman Cousins, friend and collaborator of Tanimoto.) Her acceptance speech on 24 November of that year was typical: little about herself, much about issues. Here is the second half of her speech:

> This year, the forty-fifth since the dropping of the atomic bomb, the American magazine *Playboy* published an interview in which Ishihara Shintarō, Jiyūtō Diet member, made a shockingly arrogant assertion. He expressed his opinion that the rape of Nanjing, in which according to official Chinese figures the old Japanese army massacred 300,000 Chinese, was a "story made up by the Chinese, a lie."[12] A strong reaction against this statement has arisen among Chinese living in America.
>
> The dropping of the atomic bomb, a crime against international law, is intolerable. But flat-out denying historical fact— saying that there was no rape of Nanjing, that the Chinese dreamed it up—and then on top of that bringing in America's dropping of the atomic bomb in order to absolve Japan of guilt as victimizer: that is to use Japan's *hibakusha* [atomic bomb victims] to advance one's argument through sheer force. The *hibakusha* of Hiroshima and Nagasaki are mortified.
>
> An American intellectual of good conscience has lamented, "We must not forget Pearl Harbor. But the dropping of the atomic bombs was a moral defeat for the United States." In just this way, the *hibakusha* of Hiroshima say: "We must not forget the dropping of the atomic bombs. But *hibakusha* realize that we, too, as residents of Fortress Hiroshima, cooperated in an aggressive war and provided a motive for dropping the bomb."
>
> The government and people in public life often say that Japan is the only country to have been the victim of the atomic bomb. But states aren't victims of bombs; people, including women, children, and old people, are. And the Japanese weren't the only victims; many foreigners were victims, too. The largest group of foreigners among the *hibakusha* was an estimated 70,000 Koreans.

Korean *hibakusha* ask the Japanese: "Why were Koreans swept up into another country's war and made victims of the bomb?"

When Japan annexed Korea in 1910, Koreans had their land and their language stolen on account of Japan's colonial control, and they were forced to adopt Japanese surnames. Having lost the basis of their livelihood, they were forced to emigrate to Japan and, as the war widened, to perform heavy labor; on top of all that they experienced atomic hell.

From the 1970s onward Hiroshima did not permit a monument to Korean victims to be set up within Peace Park. It was erected at the end of Honkawa Bridge opposite Peace Park. Thinking of the resentment of Korean *hibakusha*, discriminated against even in death, I wrote the poem "Out of the Stone."[13]

Antinuclear groups and even civic groups and students on school excursions protested against the city's discriminatory policy, but the mayor stubbornly held his ground. . . .

Until now, *hibakusha* of Hiroshima and Nagasaki have gone abroad to argue the cruelty of atomic bombs and to plead for the abolition of nuclear weapons, but recently victims of the war have begun to come to Japan from Asia and the Pacific to testify to the large-scale atrocities that the Japanese army committed.

Hiroshima was once Fortress Hiroshima, and today it maintains throughout the city imposing cenotaphs and ruins in memory of emperors and their army; these monuments sing of holy war. Hiroshima itself was a victim, of course, but the true Hiroshima demands an acknowledgment of Japan's war guilt and a sensitivity to the aggression and murder Japan committed. Failure on these fronts raises questions about Japan's war guilt and about its militarization as a great power since. The true Hiroshima demands that there be a "dual awareness, of Japan as victim and Japan as victimizer."

Kurihara spoke of the reactions of Asian writers: in remembering 6 August Japan should not forget its aggressions in Asia; and had more atomic bombs fallen, Japan's economy might not have recovered so quickly. Kurihara spoke of Asian fears should Japan's Self-Defense Forces be sent abroad and of a 1990 public television series in which Ōe Kenzaburō interviewed various world literary figures. In Ōe's interview with the Korean poet Kim Chi-ha, Kim stated:

I have my doubts about your theme, "Does the world remember Hiroshima?" What about the Nanjing massacre? What about the forced labor of Koreans? Without moral purity, one can't pursue the issue of responsibility. What about the Japanese attitude toward Korean *hibakusha*? Japan gave only $320 million for the medical treatment of Korean *hibakusha*. To say that the treaty between Japan and Korea settled the issue is to be extremely bureaucratic. Before asking, "Do we remember Hiroshima?" we need to ask about Japan's moral purity.

Said Kurihara:

> Kim Chi-ha's words were a response not merely to Ōe but to those who stress Hiroshima and to all Japanese.
>
> The main theme of Hiroshima is to press on from the early stage—victims arguing the cruelty of the atomic bomb—to an understanding of the essence of the nuclear culture that gave birth to the bomb. It is to broaden the issue from the destruction of people to the destruction of the globe and the destruction of the environment. It is to reflect on the fact that Japanese aggression and murder provided a motive for the dropping of the atomic bomb.
>
> The question is not whether the world remembers Hiroshima; rather, it is whether Hiroshima asks itself and others what it can do for the world. By being more world-centered, I think we may be able to restore what Kim Chi-ha called "moral purity."[14]

Kurihara Sadako remains active today. In June 1992, when I visited her in Hiroshima, she still maintained a schedule that would daunt people thirty years younger. At the end of May she had traveled to Tokyo to read a new poem at a demonstration against the sending of Self-Defense Forces on U.N. peace-keeping operations. In late June a U.N. conference on disarmament convened in Hiroshima, and Kurihara was there to leaflet and to take part in a sit-in.

Kurihara's Writings

For twenty-three years after *Kuroi tamago*, Kurihara published no books of poetry. Then in 1967 she published *Watakushi wa Hiroshima o shōgen suru* [I bear witness for Hiroshima] (Hiroshima: Shishū Kankō No Kai), and afterward came *Hiroshima: Mirai fūkei* [Hiroshima: futurescape] (Hiroshima: Shishū Kankō No Kai, 1974); *Hiroshima to iu toki* [When we say "Hiroshima"] (Tokyo: San'ichi, 1976); *Mirai wa koko kara hajimaru* [The future begins here] (Hiroshima: Shishū Kankō No Kai, 1979); *Kakujidai no dowa* [Tales for the nuclear age] (Hiroshima: Shishū Kankō No Kai, 1982); and, in 1983, the complete version of *Kuroi tamago* (Kyoto: Jinbun Shōin). In 1984 appeared *Kurihara Sadako shishū* [Poetry of Kurihara Sadako] (Tokyo: Doyō Bijutsusha, number 17 in its series of contemporary Japanese poets). That volume included selections from the earlier volumes, nine previously unpublished poems, and a long essay comparing the writers of Hiroshima and the writers of the European Holocaust.[15] In 1985 came *Hiroshima* (Hiroshima: Shishū Kankō No Kai); in 1986, *Aoi hikari ga hirameku sono mae ni* [Before the blue light flashes] (Hiroshima: Shishū Kankō No Kai); and in 1990, *Kakunaki asu e no inori o komete* [With a prayer for a nuclear-free tomorrow] (Hiroshima: Shishū Kankō No Kai).

Kurihara's first volume of essays appeared in 1970: *Dokyumento—Hiroshima nijūyonen: gendai no kyūsai* [Document—Hiroshima at twenty-four: today's redemption] (Tokyo: Shakai Shinpō). There followed *Hiroshima no genfūkei o idaite* [Embracing the atomic landscape of Hiroshima] (Tokyo: Miraisha, 1975); *Kaku, tennō, hibakusha* [Nukes, emperor, hibakusha] (Tokyo: San'ichi, 1978); *Kakujidai ni ikiru* [Life in the nuclear age] (Tokyo: San'ichi, 1982); and *Towareru Hiroshima* [Questions for Hiroshima] (Tokyo: San'ichi, 1992).

As these titles indicate, Kurihara writes on the *hibakusha* and on atomic bomb literature; the writer Ōta Yōko and the poet Shōda Shinoe (1911–65) receive her special attention. She writes about the war, about the emperor, and about the ups and downs of the antiwar movement. She comments on contemporary events in Japan and elsewhere. In short, she is part archivist-historian, part literary critic, and part activist-journalist.

A pamphlet of English translations, *The Songs of Hiroshima*, appeared in 1962, and it has gone through many printings. Apart from scattered individual poems and the essay that appeared in *Holocaust and Genocide Studies* (see n.

15), the work of Kurihara Sadako has not been available to English-language readers.[16]

What journals publish her works? Five volumes of her roughly 125 essays cover the period 1956–91; of these essays, forty appeared in newspapers and journals based in Hiroshima (*Chūgoku shinbun* alone accounted for half of these), and another nine appeared in a Nagasaki journal. Only one essay—a short 1969 piece on her single most famous poem, the relatively apolitical "Let Us Be Midwives!"—appeared in a newspaper with national distribution, the *Yomiuri*. Conspicuous by their absence are the other major national newspapers (*Asahi* and *Mainichi*) and journals of opinion (*Asahi jyanaru*, *Shisō*, *Bungei shunjū*, and the like). The specifically literary and poetic journals that publish her essays are similarly local rather than national. Kurihara is still largely shut out of the national media.

Kurihara's Ideas

Masao Miyoshi has suggested that in today's affluent Japan "the literature of critical opposition is nearly invisible."[17] He mentions Ōe Kenzaburō and a few recent feminist writers, but not Kurihara. To be sure, his subject, narrowly taken, is fiction, and Kurihara has not written fiction. But Kurihara belongs to the critical opposition; indeed, she would not have it any other way. As she stated in 1985: "Literature is not dependent upon politics; it goes ahead of politics. In every age free literature stands in opposition to the status quo."[18]

Kurihara plays important editorial and political roles in preserving and defending the heritage of Hiroshima literature and poetry, but she is not primarily a literary critic. She is a poet, composer of some four hundred poems, and author of over one hundred essays.

For Kurihara, to live is to write poetry. Kurihara's poems and essays have won her an audience, but in the most basic sense she writes for herself. In dialogue with her husband's anarchism and under the influence of the war, Kurihara's political views matured, but she could not publish; it was dangerous even to set her thoughts down in private. Kurihara herself has commented: "Even if I wrote, I couldn't publish; but I wrote because I wanted to write. Writing seemed to steady me."[19]

The end of the war brought an end to any physical danger from writing—at least until the last few years. The American Occupation exercised censorship (see below, pp. 28–33), but after 1952 Kurihara was free to publish. However, as Herbert Marcuse's concept of repressive tolerance suggests, freedom to publish does not guarantee a hearing. From 1945 through today, Kurihara has been a prophet with little honor in her own country. But honor has its disadvantages. Kurihara commented in 1987: "When things are going well, my poems become shallow. The poems I compose when I stand alone, I think, go deeper."[20]

In several poems she speaks candidly of her isolation. Here, for example, is the beginning and ending of "I'll Always Keep Singing," which she composed in 1952—during the Korean War and the concurrent remilitarization of Japan:

Despite everything, I'll keep singing.
Bald pates shining,
the unrighteous swagger about,
fill the air with the smell of rot,
raise raucous voices: amid the din,
with all my might
I'll keep singing no, no, no.

But of course Kurihara's "no" is ultimately a "yes":

The night's still dark.
Shut up within the walls of night,
walls that yield not at all,
I'll always keep singing.

Or consider "The Gilded Hearse," a poem from 1988 in which she foresees her own death:

The day is not far off when I too
will depart in that gilded hearse.
The day comes when its metal doors will close on me

and I'll depart this world forever.
Until that day
I want to blow my flute
and sing
for the sake of those alive today
and the children of the future:
"Don't turn this globe into ruins!"

At times Kurihara has despaired over the seeming in-
ability of words to move people. In "Words—Come Back to
Life!" (1968), she asks:

Words—have they no power
to bubble up from the grass roots,
make groves and forests tremble,
lay siege to the castles of the arrogant?
The words born glistening
out of that burnt-out waste where the dead sleep—
have they died?

. . .

Dead words, come back to life!
Bathed in the blood of the young,
lighted by the flames of the man who set himself afire,
the song of the dead, song without words,
calls out.

A second poem, "Leaves Blowing in the Wind" (1973), com-
pares ineffective words to dead leaves:

Standing on the corner passing out leaflets,
I appealed to people.
Leaves blowing in the wind,
my words fell on deaf ears.
Words, words, words:
I said them over and over,
but they failed to move people.

. . .

Words, words, words:
I wanted them to have force and meaning,
but I couldn't help doubting their power.
I had fallen under the spell of words,
I had fallen into the snare of words.
Words had become windblown leaves
and threatened to bury me.

Kurihara wrote the title essay of her volume *Hiroshima no genfūkei o idaite* [Embracing the atomic landscape of Hiroshima] in 1974, and it ends on a note that is as near pessimism as Kurihara ever gets in her essays. Here is its final paragraph:

> With none of its problems solved and nuclear weapons casting their shadow on the world, Japan still seeks to become an independent nuclear power. The problems of aged *hibakusha*, Korean *hibakusha*, and second-generation *hibakusha* are left unaddressed, and we don't even have confirmed figures for the dead, let alone for the population of *hibakusha*. Unless we give form to the experience of Hiroshima and Nagasaki, turn it into ideas, and universalize it, Hiroshima and Nagasaki as the experience of terror and darkness will hang in the air like the mushroom clouds, will not put down roots, will weather away. Nuclear culture objectifies the *hibakusha* experience, removes it from the realm of fact, and destroys humanity at its very roots; it is the blind alley into which the inhumane state structure has led us. And computer culture makes a mockery of human beings. Tackling antlike the vast and staggering task of destroying nuclear and computer culture, I grow weary, exhaust myself. But the atomic landscape of twenty-eight years ago does not allow me to rest.[21]

Kurihara defended Hara Tamiki's right to be left in peace and Ōta Yōko's right to stop addressing the issues of the atomic bomb, but Kurihara's indomitable spirit would not let her forsake Hiroshima and the bomb. In an essay of 1967, "Hiroshima ni chinmoku no kenri wa nai" [No right of silence for Hiroshima], she writes of soliciting signatures for a petition asking the prefecture for aid to *hibakusha*, a petition spurred by the case of a *hibakusha* patient who was dying of cancer and was piteously ill—there was cancer "all over her body," and countless injections, including male hormones, had given her a thick mustache, rough skin, and a hoarse voice. Kurihara "wanted to back away and flee," yet the patient still wanted to live. Even the doctors were astonished.

Kurihara "simply could not be persuaded" by Ōe Kenzaburō's *Hiroshima Notes* that suicide is a legitimate way out. She describes *harakiri* as "medieval" and the suicide by *harakiri* of an old *hibakusha* as "eccentric" and "crazy," lacking in the selflessness of the self-immolations of Vietnamese monks. Here is Kurihara:

> What remains forever in my mind is . . . the face of Shōda Shinoe, tears in her eyes, humming softly: "I want to live, I want to live." It is not "I will not commit suicide," but "I still want to live." A *hibakusha*, she knew the value of life from that unique experience. . . . Radiation rotted her body, but she lived with a positive attitude until the end. She had no room for a right to silence or for alienation. Even after her illness worsened and the sign "No visitors allowed" was hung on her door, she pleaded with all the people she met and urged them on.

Kurihara concludes:

> Isn't it the case that Hiroshima's cliquish anticreativity has caused the movement to abolish nuclear weapons to stagnate and has enabled the political parties to maintain control? Hiroshima is tough, positive life born from the depths of hell. . . . Hiroshima is an idea that transcends nuclear bombing. Hiroshima is the conscience of a world that does not allow nuclear bombs.[22]

Thus does Kurihara reveal her own toughness and devotion to life.

Kurihara has a positive horror of silence—both her own silence (as in "The Crow") and that of others who should speak out but don't. Kurihara devotes long essays to the silence of the *hibakusha*. Both in these essays and elsewhere, her main point is clear: "People who have witnessed such tragedy must tell of it. That is the responsibility, the duty that survivors owe to those who died." The term I have translated "tell" has a broad range of meanings, most of which apply here: convey, report, communicate; teach, make known; hand down, bequeath; and conduct, propagate.[23]

But experience alone is not enough. At the end of an essay addressed to college students in 1970, Kurihara gives this advice:

> If members of the younger generation would come down from their intellectual heights and go to where the *hibakusha* are,

speak to them not with movement language and revolutionary language but with everyday words, and summon forth from beneath their weathered surfaces the Hiroshima that even now breathes fire, I think that together they could come up with a logic by which to act. People who in the midst of daily life have lost words need to be primed before they can speak. That priming probably can only come from human kindness and trust.

She speaks then of the importance—and the limits—of experience:

> The awesome destructive power of nuclear weapons surpasses the human power of imagination. It is said that today there exist nuclear weapons sufficient to destroy every person on earth thirty-six times over, and that fact is impossible for the senses to register. Unless you flesh out ideas with experience, experience with ideas, both will decay, become mere skeletons, and make ongoing development impossible.[24]

Writing in the same vein in 1972, Kurihara invokes the famous opening exchange of Marguerite Duras's *Hiroshima Mon Amour*:

> "I saw Hiroshima." "You saw nothing." If Japanese today were to say to people from Southeast Asia, "We experienced Hiroshima," the response would surely be, "You Japanese experienced nothing. The invasion of Asia and the atomic bomb blew past you like the wind."
>
> Experience that does not take even one step beyond the closed-off, narrow experience of an individual's immediate surroundings, no matter how irreplaceable that experience is to the individual, resembles the wriggling of an octopus in an octopus pot. Experience has to rise to the level of antinuclear ideas, and ideas must descend to the depths of experience where hatreds eddy; without mutual verification, both will harden, and it will be impossible to carry forward a living movement.[25]

This emphasis on ideas makes its initial appearance in Kurihara's "Introduction" to *Kuroi tamago*.

In an essay from 1956, Kurihara addresses one aspect of the relationship between poetry and mundane reality. She writes:

Arms reductions are of course a good thing, but if modern war strategy and tactics have already shifted to highly scientific war centering on nuclear weapons, we cannot simply rejoice at mere reductions. The tests scheduled to be carried out in the middle of June that are reported to be the climax of this series of American tests are said to be for large intercontinental missiles with nuclear warheads. The newspapers reported that with successive tests the young poet who composed the line, "Nuclear bombs: don't tolerate them!" grew discouraged at the powerlessness of poems and the powerlessness of petitions and said, "I'm not going to compose any more poems."

Set aside for the moment the issue of whether the young poet is right to say that he wants or doesn't want to compose poetry according to whether it helps solve actual problems; the unbearable desperation of this young poet is probably common to all.

Massive human-killing experiments are carried out in places one cannot reach no matter how one appeals, no matter how one cries out.

Those with nuclear weapons say that by possessing them they restrain others, and that by preserving the balance they keep the peace. They say that they possess nuclear weapons for peace. Taking that verbatim and sideslipping into a peace argument, some people think optimistically that "nuclear war is total destruction that makes no distinction between friend and foe, so peaceful coexistence is the only alternative." But in the cause of peace, there is no alternative but to resolve one by one the causes of war and the preparations for war to come.[26]

If one wants peace, one should work for justice—or so Kurihara might have phrased it. And it appears that, unlike the young poet who stopped composing poetry because he doubted its effect, Kurihara herself would write regardless of effect.

Kurihara's life is an act of faith in words, but words themselves are not the goal. As she writes in the preface to *Kuroi tamago*, poetry is not "the depiction of simple sensual beauty, self-complacent emotional pain, and dark melancholy—things not real mirrored in morbid sensibilities." Poems are words, but the key element is the "unity of ideas" that must undergird the poems. That is, the beauty and force of poetry must be harnessed to ideas, and the ideas must suit the times. For Kurihara, the ideas are those of "a new humanism," and she listens intently for its footsteps. To be sure, this is Kurihara at her most didactic. Readers of *Black Eggs* will notice quickly that many of Kurihara's poems—for example, the lyrical "Record of My Passion" and the prosaic "Anesthetic Injection" in *Kuroi tamago*—do not meet her own criterion.

Take the poem for which Kurihara is most famous in Japan, "Let Us Be Midwives!" Looking back in 1983, Kurihara remembered hearing about the incident from a neighbor; a member of that woman's family was a co-worker of the brother of the midwife. (Kurihara took poetic license with the facts: the midwife survived and lived to the age of sixty-five. A later poem, "Prayer for a Nuclear-Free Tomorrow," commemorates the unveiling of a plaque at the site of the incident.) Kurihara wrote the poem "in one go." In speaking of the poem's impact, she says: "The emotion was so strong that it came out a pure crystal with no impurities. It is a poem with no apparent technique."[27] One can agree, but the theme—of indomitable will to live—hardly rises to the level of the structure of thought of which Kurihara speaks in her preface. In an essay from 1960 Kurihara commented on a critic's statement that "Let Us Be Midwives!" and "Reconstruction" were evidence of the beauty of human nature that not even atomic bombs could break:

> Paradoxically, it was not that not even the atomic bomb could break it, but that the atomic bomb blew away not only people but also the power structure that thwarted freedom for human nature; those who survived exercised human nature quite naturally. So for me the defeat meant neither collapse nor an expressionless face, but the rebirth of humanity in the depths of inhumanity. However, those who had smiled sank into a deep void.[28]

Writing in 1984, Kurihara explained herself differently:

> For me poetry is not the expression of ideas sealed off hermetically from other people, nor the solving of magic wordlike riddles, nor wordplay; it is to seek to confirm, as fellow human beings living in the nuclear age and beginning to speak to the

roots of all the people of the world, the pulse of the human heart. May that process give birth to something new!

Kurihara proceeds to introduce the element of technique that she seemed to eliminate in talking of "Let Us Be Midwives!": "In my case the techniques of poetry are my hope to express myself more deeply and more beautifully, so that I can be understood better and by more people."[29]

Writing in 1978—the passage follows immediately on her discussion of the distrust of words quoted above—Kurihara speaks of what words are for: "Words exist to seek human recovery. I firmly believe that when we call out in human words, it is possible to meet in feelings that transcend national boundaries."[30] Perhaps readers are wrong to look to the poet herself for absolute consistency in her love of words.

Kurihara has scorn for the words of most Japanese writers. In 1969 she compared Japan's postwar literature to that of France, to the great disadvantage of the former:

Postwar European literature was probably able to confront Auschwitz because of the French cultural tradition, in particular the resistance movement of *Humanité* during World War II. In the Japanese cultural tradition of literati consciousness—flowers and birds, cool breezes, and a bright moon—there was no *Humanité*, so there was no soil in which to cultivate the literature of resistance. Consequently, it was perhaps inevitable that the mainstream of Japan's postwar literature was occupied, as before, by autobiographical novels of everyday life, and that what resulted was simply the absence of a historical sense that could grasp atomic literature as the gloominess of the literature of the future.[31]

In 1978 she wrote: "Distrust of words—has it not been invited by poets who deny the meaningfulness of words, who turn words into mere artifacts, make playthings of them?"[32] And in 1983 she dismissed contemporary poets in no uncertain terms: "they write, as always, shallow poems of puns and manners and sex."[33] In response to an inquiry from me about her favorite poets then and now, Kurihara wrote in 1992:

During the war virtually without exception poets wrote poems
that contributed to the war effort, and right after the war there
were no magazines that published poetry anywhere in Japan,
which had become a bombed-out wasteland; so I had no favor-
ite poets. Now there are many poets, but none whom I partic-
ularly admire. There are particular poems I like.[34]

In 1988 a new craze swept Japan, a fascination with the
tanka of Tawara Machi, young author of *Sarada kinenbi* [Salad
anniversary]. Kurihara was not amused. In an essay entitled
"Utau koto no omosa" [The gravity of poetry], Kurihara ex-
plained why. She began by referring to *Sange*, Shōda
Shinoe's collection of *tanka* about Hiroshima, never the sub-
ject of attention in the mass media, and by comparing the
two eras, Shōda's and Tawara's, to the detriment of 1988.
Sarada kinenbi is "no more, I think, than fragments of every-
day conversation of the new people of this overripe postwar
world in which 'you and I' [a quotation from one of Tawara
Machi's *tanka*] fuse." Literary language (*bungotai*) is essential
to true *tanka*; conversational *tanka* are really short free verse.

But Kurihara's complaint is not simply a matter of form.
Kurihara quotes the two *tanka* in *Sarada kinenbi* that mention
things nuclear and writes that they represent an "over-
optimism that goes beyond lack of interest" in things nu-
clear. Nor, she suggests, is Tawara utterly unaware of the
price of this "apparent innocence":

> Living the me-ism of the postmodern is the point of departure
> for postwar thought. It is to discard all that forms the nucleus
> of human consciousness—war, nuclear weapons, extinction,
> death, concepts, ideals, the ego—and to float in the weight-
> lessness of everyday sensation.

Tawara Machi's many poems of eating are "no more than
fragments of capricious everyday life lacking in thought,
and not one poem contains inevitable tension, tight struc-
ture, discovery, or sensibility." They are "stunted, frivolous,
free of gravity."

To underline her critique (and, she writes with a pen
that drips sarcasm, "as an expression of respect for the au-
thor of *Sarada kinenbi*"), Kurihara offers some *tanka* of her

own. These *tanka*—doggerel, really—offer a startling contrast in content to Tawara Machi's *tanka* and in style to Kurihara's own *tanka* from *Kuroi tamago* (the latter contrast is difficult to convey in translation). The most startling of these *tanka* is a take-off on the poem that gave Tawara's volume its title; Kurihara replaces *sarada kinenbi* (salad anniversary) with *genbaku kinenbi* (atomic bomb anniversary):

> Because two hundred thousand
> were burned to death,
> carbonized,
> August sixth is
> atomic bomb anniversary.[35]

As Kurihara herself has written, there are striking parallels between Hiroshima literature and the literature of the European Holocaust. Both are literatures *in extremis*; both are literatures of witness. Here is a comment from 1985: "Atomic bomb poetry and prose began to be written by novelists, poets, and anonymous individuals who experienced firsthand being speechless, able only to stand dumb in the midst of mass death—written because as human beings they could not not speak of it."[36] In an essay of 1983 Kurihara quotes Paul Celan, poet of the European Holocaust:

> In the midst of the war, language remained available. . . . and if one utters this language, it was language that had been unable to escape death, language painted over with silence. In the cruelty and horror of a war in which one lost language and could only stand there dumbly, poets lived by affirming that for themselves and for others poets can write only if they believe in words, and I am one who believes that it is the very life of poets to use words that arise from human response as triggering devices to bring people together in love and peace; I wish to live, write, act, and make common cause.[37]

Kurihara lived the life of an emancipated woman—marrying for love and conviction against the desires of her family and playing an active role in literary and political circles. Relations between men and women both in literature and in life are the subject of three essays Kurihara contributed to *Chūgoku bunka* during 1946 and 1947. In the first of these, for the inaugural issue of *Chūgoku bunka*, she suggests that female suffrage, proclaimed in December 1945, is welcome but is not in itself a solution to the problems women face. Given the patriarchal family structure, a wife can enjoy at best "the freedom of a large cage."[38]

In *Kuroi tamago* "Respect for Humanity" attacks the state policy of encouraging women to have children:

> "It's state policy,
> so have children!"
> Sounds as easy as
> getting hens
> to lay more eggs.

She concludes: "women, get angry / at systematized / life and death!" One of her later poems (1985) bears the title, "Women's Principles: Life and Peace." It includes the lines: "Let's turn male principles—bullets and bombs— / into female principles—life and peace."

So "The Vine" in *Kuroi tamago* may jar some readers. In that poem, which occupies the strategic position of last of the free verse, Kurihara compares herself to a vine:

> Give me a pole tall and strong,
> and I can reach the sky; . . .
> I am a weak vine,
> but give me a pole tall and strong,
> and I can reach the sky.

"The Vine" is not dated, but it follows three poems from March 1946; thus, Kurihara likely composed it at about the same time.

Free Verse and *Tanka*

Kuroi tamago contains free verse (*shi*) and *tanka*; the later poems are all free verse. Some discussion of the two forms is in order. Japanese poetry has never relied on rhyme. Free verse, verse without syllable count or prescribed length, is a development of the nineteenth and twentieth centuries.

Kurihara's free-verse poems vary in length. "Fever," the shortest in *Kuroi tamago*, runs eight lines with no stanza breaks. "The Silkworm" runs nine lines with two stanza breaks. "Reconstruction" runs twenty-two lines in four stanzas. "War Close Up" runs thirty-nine lines in four stanzas. Stanzas can be of any length. Kurihara has written shorter and longer free verse: "River of Flames Flowing through Japan" (1959) runs 121 lines in five stanzas ranging from five to fifty-one lines.

The *shi* of *Kuroi tamago* take up many themes, ranging from reflections on relations between a husband and wife to life during the war, to events of the immediate postwar era. But none of twenty-nine *shi* deals directly with Kurihara's experience of the atomic bomb, and only two—"Let Us Be Midwives!" and "Reconstruction"—deal with 6 August at all. (Of the thirty-seven *tanka* sequences in *Kuroi tamago*, five deal with the atomic bomb, two directly, and Kurihara placed these two sequences, forty-one *tanka* in all, at the start of the *tanka* section.)

In translating Kurihara's free verse, I have preserved line count and stanza breaks. Beyond that basic replication, line-for-line translation doesn't work, nor does counting syllables. My first concern has been to make available the meaning of the free verse, but a close second concern has been to re-create the poems as poems.

Tanka are very different. *Tanka*, literally "short poems," have a history going back to the earliest Japanese verse. The syllable count for an individual *tanka* is 5–7–5–7–7, and that individual unit can be multiplied almost without end. In *Kuroi tamago* the shortest *tanka* group ("Newspaper Articles") is three poems; the longest ("Nightmare") is twenty-three. There are natural breaks between poems, but Kurihara also employs two other kinds of break: editorial comment (as in "The Day of the Atomic Bomb," between the thirteenth and fourteenth poems) and visual breaks (as in "Snowy Night," before the final two poems).

Tanka employ a set of conventions, including the repetition of set phrases for cumulative effect. Kurihara uses repetition to best effect in "City Ravaged by Flames" ["Yakeato no machi"]. The *ya-ke-a-to no* of the title is a five-syllable line that starts ten of the nineteen poems, including all five poems of section two; it appears elsewhere in three poems. *Yakeato* itself involves something of a play on words, another *tanka* convention. *Ato* can mean both "mark," "trace," or "ruin" and "after." Thus, the phrase can mean both "the burned ruins" and "after the fire." Kurihara writes it with the character for the former in all but four cases (poems 4, 12, 13, 17); in those four cases she uses *kana* (the Japanese syllabary). I have translated it throughout as "ravaged by flames."

In Japanese, *tanka* are usually printed in a single vertical line thirty-one syllables long. Translators into English have tried various arrangements: one line, three lines, four lines, and five lines. Since syllables and their significance differ in English and in Japanese, other factors must be considered. I have translated Kurihara's *tanka* into five lines, preserving syllable count only where I could do so without harming poetic flow.

After *Kuroi tamago* Kurihara published no more *tanka*, which was in part a political decision. Writing in 1960, the critic Kuwabara Takeo argued that the day of *tanka* was past, and Kurihara agreed.[39] In recent correspondence with me, Kurihara wrote: "For about a year after *Kuroi tamago* I composed *tanka*, but *tanka* are small in scope, and there are restrictions as to content, so I stopped composing them and came to express myself in free verse and essays."[40] It speaks eloquently of Kurihara's political commitment that one so adept at *tanka* would forego the pleasures of a verse form that had given expression to her deepest emotions.

Kuroi tamago begins with free verse and ends with *tanka*. The free verse are arranged neither in chronological order nor according to content. The *tanka* follow a somewhat clearer pattern. The first nine sequences date from the end of the war; the later sequences move generally backward in time. The Selected Later Poems follow my arrangement, not Kurihara's: within each section they move chronologically, from earlier to later poems.

Poetry reveals the poet in many ways, and Kurihara's poetry is extraordinarily honest, not simply about "ideas" (the antiwar poems like "From All the Battlefronts") but also about intensely personal events and issues ("Overgrown Garden," "Do Not Open," "Fatigue" among the free verse; "Miscellany," "Record of My Passion," "Cactus Flowers" among the *tanka*). "The Silkworm" speaks both of her past and of her future. It mentions nothing but a silkworm, but in the second stanza the silkworm "reflected on the several molts of its life till then," and, in the third, what the silkworm has to spin is not silk but ideas. There had been molts in Kurihara's life before 1945; there would be molts after 1945. There have been periods of apparent inactivity, but ideas and poetry have always emerged.

Some poems in *Kuroi tamago* foreshadow Kurihara's later work in important ways. "Korean Maiden," a straightforward tribute to the beauty and grace of a member of an underclass in Japan, prepares readers for Kurihara's later concern with Japan as oppressor, both at home and abroad. In "Basking in the Sun" she invokes the tale of Diogenes and Alexander; in "The Fox's Gold Coins" she uses Japanese folk tales. Some of her most effective later poems— "Nippon: Piroshima" (1971), "His Majesty Has Donkey's Ears" (1980), and "Hiroshima and the Emperor's New Clothes" (1981)—make effective use of European and Japanese mythology.

Occupation Censorship and *Kuroi tamago*

Before and during the war Kurihara Sadako wrote poems she didn't dare publish; government censorship and thought control were so strong as to make it an act of courage even to commit such poems to paper. After the war Kurihara faced a new situation: foreign authority. There was no physical danger, but there was continued censorship. And the Occupation censorship covered its own tracks (under Japanese censorship editors routinely indicated passages where censorship had caused deletions), which made it more insidious if less life-threatening.[41]

One of the areas of sensitivity for the censors who worked for the Supreme Commander for the Allied Powers (SCAP) was the atomic bomb. Before SCAP regulations went into effect on 18 September 1945, Ōta Yōko published her first report on the bomb, "A Flash As at the Bottom of the Sea."[42] But thereafter all the Hiroshima writers—Ōta, Hara Tamiki, and Tōge Sankichi—encountered in varying degrees the heavy hand of the censors. Kurihara Sadako was no exception.

The inaugural issue of *Chūgoku bunka* (March 1946) provided the occasion for Kurihara Sadako's first encounter with the Occupation censors. Her husband was listed as the individual responsible, and thus it fell to him to stick the manuscript and some food in a knapsack and set off for Fukuoka in Kyushu. (SCAP divided Japan into three parts, and Hiroshima fell under the jurisdiction of Fukuoka.) The censors deleted some passages but "made no major deletions."[43] That was prepublication censorship.

Once the journal appeared, it underwent postpublication censorship, this time by the Civil Censorship Division stationed in Kure. Summoned to Kure, Tadaichi was grilled: Did he not know of paragraphs 3 and 4 of the press code? Paragraph 3 read as follows: "There shall be no false or destructive criticism of the Allied Powers." Paragraph 4 was closely related: "There shall be no destructive criticism of the Allied Forces of Occupation and nothing that might invite mistrust or resentment of these troops."[44] According to Sadako, remembering in 1983, Tadaichi replied: "I trust that the United States is a democratic country. For a democratic country to set up a system of censorship, and then, once a publication has been censored and cleared for publication, to make it once again the target of complaint: that is worse than Japan's prewar and wartime censorship. It absolutely wipes out my trust in American democracy." Despite the summons to Kure, no punishment ensued; Tadaichi was warned, however, "In no sense may you write something to the effect that the horrors of the atomic bomb still continue even after the blast." Sadako declares that *Chūgoku bunka* complied.[45]

When it came to *Kuroi tamago*, Kurihara Sadako sent the manuscript off for prepublication censorship on 20 July 1946. The censors approved publication provided that Kurihara delete four poems in whole (two free-verse poems, one *tanka* sequence) or in part (one free-verse poem). She printed 3,000 copies privately (they sold for five *yen* plus thirty *sen* for postage); the volume was typeset, not mimeographed, a rarity at the time.

Kurihara writes about the censorship of *Kuroi tamago* in her preface to the 1983 edition, translated with this volume. Therefore I will add here only a few comments drawn from an essay Kurihara wrote in 1983. First, it is difficult to understand the motives of the censors in deleting the first eleven lines of "War Close Up," an antiwar poem by almost any definition. Rather than print the poem in abbreviated form, Kurihara deleted the whole thing. The censors also deleted "What Is War?" Here is Kurihara's comment:

> During the war I hesitated even to record such works in manuscript notes. I was surprised that such works were deleted by the Occupation army. . . . I could understand its concealing its own atomic crimes, but why would it delete and conceal criticism of the Japanese army's war demagoguery and the atrocities against women and children that it carried out in occupied areas of mainland China? I inferred that the authorities feared that the American army was committing in its occupied area . . . the same kind of atrocities and violence against women . . . and that these poems would reinforce that image.[46]

The dust jacket illustration is a photograph of page fifteen of *Kuroi tamago* after Kurihara had submitted it to the American Occupation in July 1946 for prepublication censorship. The page contains the poem "What Is War?"; the title is at the right, not crossed out. "What Is War?" first appeared in print in 1983, thirty-eight years after it had been censored.

The third free-verse poem to incur the red ink of the
censors was "Handshake." This decision was a surprise to
Kurihara and remains a surprise today. A light poem written
from the point of view of Japanese children and showing no
hostility whatsoever to the American troops, "Handshake"
may have fallen afoul of American sensitivities on the issue
of fraternization. Kurihara states:

> I lived then as now in Gion-chō Nagatsuka, four kilometers
> from ground zero; there were thatched-roof farmhouses here
> and there, and in the heat of the bomb several had instantly
> gone up in flames. People said that Occupation soldiers had
> come to see those houses. Occupation soldiers had also come
> by jeep to a neighboring farmhouse, and those people said,
> "They brought lots of beer and candy. They were very nice;
> that stuff about British and American demons was a big lie."
> Far from being criticism of the Occupation army, "Handshake"
> was a poem from the point of view of children welcoming
> American soldiers; the authoritarianism of the Occupation
> army probably disapproved of yellow "Jap" children of the
> defeated enemy asking to shake hands.[47]

The censors deleted all eleven poems of the *tanka* group
"The Fall of Paris—Hitler." Kurihara herself finds it "inexpli-
cable" that the censors reacted against a poem criticizing
Hitler's barbarity.

Although they passed prepublication censorship, Kuri-
hara decided on her own to delete nine additional *tanka*: the
last five of "The Day of the Atomic Bomb" and all four of
"The Surrender." The former depict *hibakusha* in flight, with
the time unspecified, and Kurihara may have taken to heart
the censors' warning to Tadaichi not to deal with the contin-
uing effects of the bomb. "The Surrender" speaks of the
poet's ambiguous feelings toward the occupiers.

Why delete these poems when the censors had already
cleared them? Here is Kurihara's statement of 1983:

> When I published the censored version [of *Kuroi tamago*], I
> myself deleted the last five poems of "The Day of the Atomic
> Bomb" and all four poems of "The Surrender." Today readers

may find this strange. But despite the fact that we published the special issue of *Chūgoku bunka* on the atomic bomb precisely as the prepublication censors instructed, we had a bitter experience with the postpublication censors: arbitrarily being checked and reprimanded. In the case of *Kuroi tamago*, then, I deleted those *tanka* myself despite the fact that the poems had passed prepublication censorship. I exercised excessive self-regulation. In this way too the psychological pressures that the system of censorship exerted on authors and publishers manifested themselves.[48]

In early 1948, eighteen months after the censors passed *Kuroi tamago* with deletions, two events caused concern to the Occupation's censors: the Tokyo war crimes trial, then nearing its climax, and the dedication of Peace Park in April 1948. The Occupation's Civil Information and Education Section debated "measures designed to counter Japanese attitudes in connection with the atom bombing of Hiroshima and Nagasaki and ultra-nationalist propaganda aired during the war crimes trials." A draft document ("Subject: War Guilt Information Program," 6 February 1948) summarized activities to date, largely the dissemination of material about Japanese war crimes and the progress of the Tokyo war crimes trial. But:

> On the basis of oral reports only from G-2 (CIS), this section understands that:
> a. Some individuals and groups in Japan, inspired by the writings and public remarks of certain scientists, clergymen, authors, journalists and professional do-gooders in the United States, are branding the atom bombings of Hiroshima and Nagasaki as "atrocities." There is also a growing feeling among some of these Americans, reflected in corresponding sentiments among certain Japanese, that whatever educational or philanthropic movements are undertaken in Hiroshim[a] with American funds should be done in a spirit of "atonement" for the alleged atrocity.

The document concluded:

> (3) It is the consensus that the Tojo trials [the Tokyo war crimes trial] and the Hiroshima-Nagasaki "atrocities" properly should be considered as coming under the heading of "war guilt."

Treatment, however, may vary in specific methods as outlined in the following plan.

Under "Specific Methods," it suggested that the Press and Publications Unit "send a press representative to the dedication ceremonies scheduled for April 1948 at Hiroshima to encourage correct interpretation by the Japanese press," and that for radio "a special CIE radio representative" be sent for the same purpose.

And yet Kurihara Sadako will have little to do with the neo-conservative attack on American censorship. That attack is associated most closely with the critic Etō Jun. Etō has written in particular about Yoshida Mitsuru's *Requiem for Battleship Yamato*.[49] But writing in 1983 Kurihara had this to say: "What I wish to stress here is that although there are those who argue that postwar democracy under Occupation censorship was a delusion, on the contrary for those who overcame censorship and made democratization a fact, postwar democracy was by no means a delusion."[50] Her feet always on the ground, poet Kurihara is closer to reality than critic Etō. In any case, censorship ended with the Occupation. It was not a factor in any of her later poems.

The Texts

In the "Preface" to the 1983 edition, Kurihara traces the publication history of *Kuroi tamago*. There are two editions: the censored version she published at her own expense in 1946 and the complete edition of 1983. The only significant differences between the two are the following: first, censorship left the first edition less than complete; second, in the complete edition Kurihara added brief notes and dates to some of the poems. For these and the later poems I have added further notes, which include dates of composition, where available, and some indication of context. The dates of composition come from Kurihara herself, for this translation; the notes come in part from Kurihara's other published writings and in part from Kurihara for this translation.

I have arranged the later poems thematically: poems that are particularly revealing of the poet's life, poems that relate directly to 6 August, poems about postwar Japanese politics and life, and so on. Within these groupings, I have arranged the poems in chronological order. But the groupings are arbitrary at best. Kurihara the poet is present in all her poems; poems that speak of 6 August are also poems about nuclear weapons; and poems that attack American bases in Japan are also an attack on postwar Japan. Readers should remain aware that the grouping is mine, not Kurihara's.

For the past dozen years I have studied the literature of Hiroshima. I began my study of *Kuroi tamago* by translating the poems that dealt with the atomic bomb. Some of the other poems—notably the title poem "Black Eggs"— seemed not to translate well. Others—especially a few of the *tanka* sequences—seemed of secondary importance. But as I worked my way into the world of Kurihara's poetry, I was struck with its breadth and depth and beauty. I realized also how different it is from what the prevailing stereotypes lead us to expect. Further, I saw how far Kurihara's world is from the world of those on whom Japanese and American critics alike have focused their attention. I came to believe that *Kuroi tamago* taken as a whole is a work of significance as poetry, as intellectual and social history, and as a waysta- tion in the career of Kurihara Sadako. I came to see in the later poems both development on the base Kurihara estab- lished in *Kuroi tamago* and intrinsic merit.

Kurihara lives in the nuclear age: "The human aliena- tion of nukes and pollution is the very essence of the nuclear age; it is the end phase of a modern science and culture that are contemptuous of people and treat them as objects." She strives to universalize the *hibakusha* experience and make of it a fundamental element of modern thought, to use it in the cause of human liberation from things nuclear. Thus, Hiro- shima and Nagasaki become an indispensable part of to- day's ideas, part not of the past but of the future:

Hiroshima is by no means something that happened in the past. As the cruelest end point of Fortress Hiroshima, Hiroshima is a futurescape in which we see where militarism leads, where the arms race leads, their destination; it is humankind's greatest blind spot that serves notice to the world.[51]

In the afterword to her 1976 volume of poetry, Kurihara wrote:

When people actually feel the terror of our current nuclear world, can they control the madness? If people do not succumb to madness, it may be that they are avoiding the nukes by means of emotional paralysis. All the people in the world, including even innocent babies asleep in their cradles, are captives of the nukes. So there is no human liberation without liberation from the nukes.[52]

Writing in 1970 of Japanese opposition to nuclear weapons, Kurihara began an essay with these words:

It is no exaggeration to say that the twenty-five years of Hiroshima—in a word, the period since the atomic taboo that began with the Occupation army's press code—have been years of progress for citizen resistance against the attempts of the two governments—Japan and the United States—to cover up the true facts of the atomic bombings and to dispel the nuclear allergy.[53]

We can say much the same of Kurihara's life and work. In conditions ranging from censorship to relative toleration, over not twenty-five years but nearly fifty, with a persistence and application only the mural painters Maruki Iri and Maruki Toshi can equal, Kurihara Sadako has kept the faith. In the process, she has produced a body of poetry that will surely stand as one of the major artistic testimonies to life in the nuclear age.

Notes

1. For biographical data see the chronology in Kurihara Sadako, *Kurihara Sadako shishū* [Poems of Kurihara Sadako], *Nihon gendaishi bunko* 17 (Tokyo: Doyō Bijutsusha, 1984), 155–60, and a series of sixteen brief articles (unsigned) in Hiroshima's *Chūgoku shinbun* beginning 17 July 1987.

Kuroi tamago ("Black Eggs") is the title of a poem of November 1942, and Kurihara used it as the title of her 1946 volume of poetry that includes the poem "Black Eggs." Now, *Black Eggs* is the title of this translation of the 1946 volume *Kuroi tamago* and many of Kurihara's later poems. To avoid confusion, *Kuroi tamago* refers to the 1946 volume of poetry (and its 1983 reissue), "Black Eggs" to the poem, and *Black Eggs* to this volume.

2. "Sensō to kakumeiteki romanchishizumu no hazama de" [Caught between war and revolutionary romanticism] (August 1990), in *Towareru Hiroshima* [Questions for Hiroshima] (Tokyo: San'ichi, 1992), 158.

3. *Chūgoku shinbun*, 17 July 1987. The chronology in *Kurihara Sadako shishū* gives 26 December 1931 as the date of her "marriage," but in a later essay Kurihara writes of an "illegal marriage" at the end of 1931. It was in February 1932 that she nearly sailed for Brazil. "Sensō to kakumeiteki romanchishizumu," 153–54.

4. Kurihara Sadako, "*Kuroi tamago* to watakushi no sensō-genbaku-haisen taiken—kaisetsu ni kaete" [*Black Eggs* and my experience of war, atomic bomb, and defeat], in *Kuroi tamago: kanzenban* [Black Eggs: the complete edition] (Tokyo: Jinbun Shoin, 1983), 135–36.

5. Hosoda Tamiki, "Jo" [Preface], in *Kuroi tamago*, 10. (Hosoda's preface is not translated in this volume.) Compare Kurihara on her "progress during the war," in *Kuroi tamago*, 132–34.

6. *Nihon no genbaku bungaku* [The atomic bomb literature of Japan], vol. 15 (Tokyo: Horupu, 1983), 38–40.

7. The person who fell from the sky was Hara Tamiki; the person who rose up into the sky was Nagaoka.

8. "Hankaku ishiki no saikōchiku o—daiikkai genbaku mondai sōgō kenkyūkai no kiroku" [Toward the reconstitution of antinuclear consciousness—record of the first meeting of the general study group on the atomic bomb issue], in *Kaku jidai ni ikiru* [Life in the nuclear age] (Tokyo: San'ichi, 1982), 228.

9. Masao Miyoshi, *Off Center* (Cambridge: Harvard University Press, 1991), 172.

10. "Shi ni yoru Shōwashi" [Showa history through poetry], in *Towareru Hiroshima*, 258–59.

11. Kurihara discusses the media coverage of the emperor's death in "Tennō hōdō o megutte" [On the coverage of the emperor] (January 1989), in *Towareru Hiroshima*, 106–12. On the threats, see "Jōkyō o sōshutsu-suru" [Creating the conditions] (January 1992), in *Towareru Hiroshima*, 26–27.

12. "Interview with Shintaro Ishihara," *Playboy*, October 1990, p. 63.

13. In her speech Kurihara read this poem; for my translation, see below, pp. 283–84.

14. "Towareru Hiroshima" [Questions for Hiroshima], in *Towareru Hiroshima*, 163–75.

15. "Aushubuittsu to Hiroshima no bungaku" [The literature of Auschwitz and Hiroshima] is available in my translation in *Holocaust and Genocide Studies* 7.1 (Spring 1993): 77–106.

16. There is no complete bibliography of Kurihara's publications. The chronology in *Kurihara Sadako shishū*, 155–60, is very useful but is now ten years out of date.

17. Miyoshi, *Off Center*, 26.

18. *Chūgoku shinbun*, 26 October 1985.

19. *Chūgoku shinbun*, 8 July 1987.

20. *Chūgoku shinbun*, 23 July 1987.

21. "Hiroshima no genfūkei o idaite—watakushi no sengo rekishi" [Embracing the atomic landscape of Hiroshima—my postwar history], in *Hiroshima no genfūkei o idaite*, 253.

22. "Hiroshima ni chinmoku no kenri wa nai" [No right of silence for Hiroshima], in *Dokyumento—Hiroshima nijūyonen*, 276–77. Kurihara uses Chinese characters for the first Hiroshima in this final paragraph, denoting the actual Hiroshima; for the other Hiroshimas she uses *katakana* syllables, denoting her own—ideal—Hiroshima.

23. The two essays are "Hiroshima ni chinmoku," 268–85, and "Hibakusha naze chinmoku suru ka," in *Hiroshima no genfūkei o idaite*, 191–98. The quotation is from "Hachi.roku no imi suru mono" [What 6 August means] (July 1968), in *Hiroshima no genfūkei o idaite*, 181.

24. "Tsuranuku shimin no hangenbaku" [The continuity of the citizen antinuclear movement] (5 August 1970), in *Hiroshima no genfūkei o idaite*, 54.

25. "Genbaku taiken no konnichi-teki imi" [The contemporary meaning of the experience of the atomic bomb], in *Hiroshima no genfūkei o idaite*, 147–48. *Hiroshima Mon Amour* is the inspiration also for Kurihara's poem "Hiroshima o mita" ("I Saw Hiroshima"; see below, p. 208).

26. "Gurō-sarete iru ningen: suibaku jikken of megutte" [Humankind mocked: on the hydrogen bomb tests] (August 1956), in *Dokyumento—Hiroshima nijūyonen*, 18–19.

27. *Chūgoku shinbun*, 10 July 1987.

28. "Hiroshima no hanshō to kentō" [Hiroshima: reflection and examination] (October 1960), in *Dokyumento—Hiroshima nijūyonen*, 230–31. Kurihara has discussed "Let Us Be Midwives!" many times. Most useful are "Hiroshima: jigoku no soko no tanjō [Birth in Hiroshima, the depths of hell] (5 August 1969), in *Dokyumento—Hiroshima nijūyonen*, 9–14; *Kakujidai no dōwa*, 50–51; "Seitotachi no futatsu no bunshū" [Two collections by schoolchildren] (February 1988), in *Towareru Hiroshima*, 93–99; and "Shi ni yoru Shōwashi" [Shōwa history through poems] (June 1989), in *Towareru Hiroshima*, 249–52.

29. "Tasha to watakushi o musubu shi o" [Toward poems that link others and me], in *Shi to eiga zuishoshū* [Miscellany: poetry and movies] (Tokyo: Shi Tsūshinsha, 1984), 41.

30. "Hiroshima no shi no keifu to shi ni yoru hangenbaku undō" [The genealogy of Hiroshima poems and the anti atomic-bomb movement through poetry], in *Mirai wa koko kara hajimaru* [The future starts here] (Hiroshima: Shishū Kankō No Kai, 1979), 61.

31. "Hiroshima no bungaku o megutte—Aushubuittsu to Hiroshima" [On Hiroshima literature—Auschwitz and Hiroshima], in *Dokyumento—Hiroshima nijūyonen*, 214–15.

32. "Hiroshima no shi no keifu," 61.

33. *"Kuroi tamago* to watakushi," 141.

34. Kurihara Sadako to Richard H. Minear, 15 May 1992.

35. "Utau koto no omosa," in *Towareru Hiroshima*, 104–5.

36. *Chūgoku shinbun*, 19 October 1985.

37. *"Kuroi tamago* to watakushi," 145. Kurihara is dependent upon the Japanese translation of Lawrence Langer's *The Holocaust and the Literary Imagination*; perhaps for that reason she conflates Celan and Langer's comments on Celan.

38. "Atarashiki ren'ai to kekkon e no enkei" [New love and marriage: a distant prospect], *Chūgoku bunka* (March 1946), 42.

39. *"Kuroi tamago* to watakushi," 124.

40. Kurihara Sadako to Richard Minear, 15 May 1992.

41. On Occupation censorship and the bomb, see Monica Braw, *The Atomic Bomb Suppressed: American Censorship in Occupied Japan* (Armonk, NY: M.E. Sharpe, 1991).

42. "Umizoko no yō na hikari," *Asahi shinbun*, 30 August 1945; reprinted in *Ōta Yōko shū*, vol. 2 (Tokyo: San'ichi, 1982), 275–80.

43. *"Kuroi tamago* to watakushi," 120.

44. The text of the entire ten points is available in Braw, *The Atomic Bomb Suppressed*, 41.

45. *"Kuroi tamago* to watakushi," 121–22.

46. *"Kuroi tamago* to watakushi," 128.

47. *"Kuroi tamago* to watakushi," 129–30.

48. *"Kuroi tamago* to watakushi," 131.

49. Etō Jun, "Tozasareta gengo kūkan: senryōgun no ken'etsu to sengo Nihon" [Sealed-off linguistic space: Occupation army censorship and postwar Japan], *Shokun* 14.2 (February 1982): 34–109 and later essays. See Richard H. Minear, ed. and trans., *Requiem for Battleship Yamato*, by Yoshida Mitsuru (Seattle: University of Washington, 1985), xxxi-xxxii. Also useful is Marlene Mayo, "Literary Reorientation in Occupied Japan: Incidents of Civil Censorship," in Ernestine Schlant and J. Thomas Rimer, eds., *Legacies and Ambiguities: Postwar Fiction and Culture in West Germany and Japan* (Washington, D.C.: Woodrow Wilson Center, 1991), 135–61.

50. *"Kuroi tamago* to watakushi," 122.

51. "Genten to genten" [Where we began and where we are today] (15 August 1973), in *Hiroshima no genfūkei o idaite*, 186; "Atogaki: kaku to tennō no zettaisei kara no kaihō o" [Afterword: toward liberation from the absolutism of nukes and the emperor] (March 1978), in *Kaku, tennō, hibakusha*, 229; "Genbaku ireihi to Yasukuni jinja" [The atomic cenotaph and Yasukuni shrine] (July 1974), in *Hiroshima no genfūkei o idaite*, 242.

52. "Atogaki" [Afterword], in *Hiroshima to iu toki*, 192.

53. "Tsuranuku shimin no hangenbaku" [The continuity of the citizen antinuclear movement] (5 August 1970), in *Hiroshima no genfūkei o idaite*, 55.

PART ONE

BLACK EGGS

Foreword

THIS VOLUME is a complete edition of *Kuroi tamago*, the collection of free verse and *tanka* I composed in the period from 1940 through 1945, from before the Pacific War to the early days after the defeat.

In and around Hiroshima, in the year after the defeat, as the shock of the atomic bomb still reverberated, a cultural movement got under way that aimed at peace and democratic creativity; it launched the journal *Chūgoku bunka* (Hiroshima culture) with a special issue on the atomic bomb. In August 1946, as part of that movement, I published 3,000 copies of *Kuroi tamago*.

At the time, Japan's press was under the control of the Occupation army. All printed matter—even advertisements—had to pass censorship; what the Occupation army found inconvenient was suppressed, or deletions and changes of wording were demanded. The censors made partial deletions in the inaugural issue of *Chūgoku bunka*, and *Kuroi tamago*, too, which I published privately, had three free-verse poems and eleven *tanka* deleted. Moreover, fearing postpublication censorship, I myself deleted nine *tanka*, leaving twenty-nine free-verse poems and 250 *tanka*.

Of the two galley proofs I presented to the Occupation army for the censors to use, one was sent back to me with the parts to be deleted marked in red pencil; but in the confusion of the postwar era I lost that copy, and I was able to recall only vaguely what *Kuroi tamago* looked like before censorship. For a long time that fact weighed on my mind.

Beginning roughly at the end of the 1960s, research on the Occupation era began to flourish, and *Chūgoku bunka* and *Kuroi tamago*, both of which had been out of print, attracted attention. In 1975 I learned from Sodei Rinjirō, then conducting research on the Occupation era, that among the vast collection of materials on censorship assembled at the University of Maryland's McKeldin Library he had found galleys of *Kuroi tamago* with the deletions clearly marked. In 1982 Horiba Kiyoko, a poet from Hiroshima Prefecture and a specialist on Takamure Itsue, went to the United States and had photocopies of the McKeldin Library's *Kuroi tamago* made for me, and in October 1982, after an interval of thirty-six years, I saw the original *Kuroi tamago* once again.

As I read those galleys, my thoughts went back to the wartime years when I composed these works and to the chain of events leading up to their publication at my own expense. Thus, I came to want to set those events down, restore the deletions, and publish a complete version. (In May 1981 I had reissued *Chūgoku bunka*'s special issue on the atomic bomb.)

This book of poetry includes thirty-two free-verse poems and 270 *tanka*. When I read them now, I cringe with embarrassment. Still, in the madness of war I was able to look at the war with clear, even if naive, eyes and to set down antiwar thoughts and write of the calamity of the atomic bomb. That is evidence of the progress I had made as a young woman, and *Kuroi tamago* is the starting point for the development of my postwar ideas.

Today, when much of the reality of Occupation censorship is shrouded in darkness, this volume perhaps sheds a bit of light. And it also provides food for thought about freedom of speech and thought during the war and during the Occupation.

I received the proofs from Ms. Horiba during a period in which anger at home grew, as did protest in neighboring nations, over the Ministry of Education's certification of textbooks. As a result, I felt all the more strongly that I wanted to place this book before the public.

Generations that did not experience the war now constitute more than half the population, and the defeat and the

Occupation have receded into the distance. But as we face
an age that we might term a "new prewar era," I think of the
continuity that links the dark and grim age in which the
Japanese people experienced war, the age of defeat and Oc-
cupation, with our current age. I will be happy if one person
learns the lessons of history from this book, and happier still
if many—particularly members of younger generations—
learn these lessons.

—June 1983

Introduction

POEMS AND POETS: people greet them with scorn and
poke fun at them. Why is that?

Because people take the realm of poetry to be the depiction of simple sensual beauty, self-complacent emotional
pain and dark melancholy—things not real mirrored in morbid sensibilities. If poetry required only a unique sensitivity
and dreamy beauty, then hysterics and the mentally ill
would necessarily be great poets. In fact, the pictures such
people draw and the words they write are very similar to
art, but they are not art. Why not?

Because they have no unity of ideas. If it were merely a
matter of portraying emotional pain and unreal beauty, then
poetry would be no more than beautiful chatter. Behind the
emotions of human life lie the ideas that are the essential
pillar of human life.

Emotions are not simply emotions. Feudal emotions normally well up from feudal ideas; free and unconventional
emotions are born from free ideas.

Even during the war I wrote poems that spoke through
and through of my ideas—freedom and love and a peaceful
society, a longing for a society not based on power. At a time
when people were composing poems that glorified war, I was
off in a corner hoping for a world without war. And now the
day has come when the fighting has ended and the world is to
be knit together anew. People must be united even more
strongly by love. Yet what I come into contact with, for the
most part, is coarse and bleak, and I weep bitter tears.

[In his Introduction, not translated here] Hosoda Tamiki
described my poems as "poems that sing of boundless

love," but in searching for boundless love, I always weep bitter tears.

Yet the real tragedy would be a total absence of ideas, and that is not the case here; so even as I weep bitter tears, I shall have faith and go on searching.

Finally, I wish to express profound gratitude to Mr. Hosoda. By writing his preface, he has lent distinction to this collection of poems; I realize that this collection cannot withstand severe criticism, yet he was kind enough to encourage me, naked though I am. I thank him.

—GION, MARCH 1946

FREE VERSE

BLACK EGGS

My conceptions: like sterile eggs,

will they never hatch

no matter how long, how long, I sit on them?

O black eggs I'm incubating in my heart of hearts:

won't the day ever come

when you spread your wings and fly?

How everyone will praise you

when you break through your hard shells and spread your
      wings!

O birds promising bliss, like birds of paradise:

spread your wings! spread your wings!

—November 1942

The dates and occasional notes to the poems were not part of the first (1946)
edition; the poet added them to the complete edition of 1983. This transla-
tion gives month and year but not day. All notes are the poet's except for
those that begin with the translators initials, RHM.

WAR CLOSE UP

—On hearing over the radio a simulation of the
sounds of battle

Stirring bugles! Rousing martial music!
Announcers reporting victory as if possessed,
fanning, fanning the passions of battle!
Masters of state magic appearing one after the other,
adroitly spreading poisoned words
to block all recourse to reason!
Artistic expression turned wholly into state magic!

Our army advances, advances, advances toward the enemy:
boots, rifles, bombs, cannon.
The rumble of tanks moving forward.
The sudden sinking of enemy ships.
A radio broadcast simulating the sounds of battle.
A hymn to war booming to Heaven,
sung by pious men and women
who worship this cruel idol called war.
Ah, so mysterious that a puff
addles even completely independent spirits—
the narcotic of patriotism!!
the sophistry of race!!

On the beautiful islands and vast continents
that lie scattered over the globe,
great landholders soon appear and draw boundaries:
from here to here—my country.
They fight and increase their holdings or lose them.
Driven by boundless greed, they make war again and again.
They instill hatred in the people born there
and drive them into battle.

On high-sounding pretexts tailored to each occasion,

they raise high the banners: Our cause is just;
  our war is holy.

Justice becomes the password of thieves.

They square their shoulders: "Annihilate
  the evil enemy

and secure world peace."

They howl out:

"Fight to the last man, the last woman

even if it takes ten years, a hundred years."

Then the martial music of the magicians
  sounds still louder,

and fanatic bull-headed patriots

roar and revel;

completely bewitched, the people sing as one:

"Let me die by the side of my Sovereign!"

    —AUGUST 1942

Prepublication censorship deleted the first eleven lines. Because that action cut off the opening of the poem, I did not include it in the 1946 edition.

RHM: The final line of the poem is a line of a *Man'yōshū* poem (4094) that became a wartime song, "Umi yukaba." On the fanaticism of the wartime radio announcers, see "*Kuroi tamago* to watakushi," 134–35.

Night falls gently
on an earth that panted so for breath during the day,
and stars appear, brilliantly made up,
     each following her sister.
Moment by moment they become brighter
and sparkle with passion.
as if gazing on their lovers.
The dew that settles on my forehead as I look up at them—
their tears?
The great feast of the sky, spread out each evening.
Above the heads of those who sleep, so gaudy—
like a dream and yet real.

THE FOX'S GOLD COINS

My heart is lonely and sealed off,
it tries to converse with no one.
Not a single person speaks any more
of life in all its freshness and reality.
People are fanatic about the war,
and the world has become a vast insane asylum.
Thrust sane into its midst,
I am lost.
When from time to time I let slip a sigh,
it is a poor mother whose son died in battle
who sends me a sad glance and a "me too."
Raving lunatics laugh aloud
even when sons and husbands die in battle,
boast of silly Orders of the Golden Kite—
gold coins from a fox,
and venerate their dead as gods.
Hereabouts
this is the highest virtue.

—AUGUST 1942

RHM: The Order of the Golden Kite was awarded for outstanding valor to servicemen or their survivors. A golden kite had perched on the bow of Emperor Jinmu, the legendary conqueror who led the march eastward into Yamato. See also "The Day the Shōwa Era Ends" (below). In Japanese folklore, foxes caught by humans often buy their freedom by offering their captors gold coins. However, the gold soon turns into worthless leaves (one standard gold coin was called a "leaf"). Kurihara discusses this poem in "*Kuroi tamago* to watakushi," 136–37.

WHAT IS WAR?

I do not accept war's cruelty.
In every war, no matter how beautifully dressed up,
I detect ugly, demonic intent.
And I abhor those blackhearted people
who, not involved directly themselves,
constantly glorify war and fan its flames.
What is it that takes place
when people say "holy war," "just war"?
Murder. Arson. Rape. Theft.
The women who can't flee take off their skirts
    before the enemy troops
and beg for mercy—do they not?
In fields where the grain rustles in the breeze,
sex-starved soldiers chase the women,
like demons on the loose.
At home they are good fathers, good brothers, good sons,
but in the hell of battle,
they lose all humanity
and rampage like wild beasts.

—OCTOBER 1942

This poem was censored in its entirety.

FROM ALL THE BATTLEFRONTS

—Imagining the day peace comes

The day the soldiers return from all the battlefronts,
sunburnt, covered with dust, crawling with lice, bloody.
The day they return to fathers and mothers,
        wives and children, brothers.
From trenches over there,
from trenches here,
louder than any battle cry,
a great cheer wells up.
Each side calls across to the other:
"Hey, a great day!"
Peace, peace: the day
people once again are brought together.
A day earlier,
and those men wouldn't have died in battle.
These others wouldn't have groaned in pain, all smeared
        with blood.
Ah, four or five days earlier,
and lots of comrades would have made it through uninjured!
Ah, four or five days later,
and we too might be dead.
Ah, peace, peace.
The day the soldiers return from all the battlefronts,
a tide receding, ever homeward.
The day they come marching home.

—AUGUST 1943

ONCE MORE, THE SUN

When in former times
from ramparts high and strong
our ancestors defended the lands they held in common,
the sun shone brightly.

But hellish ideas
gradually became the black smoke of munitions factories
        and threatened to cloud the sun,
to rise on wings, cross the sea,
become fire bombs and set human civilization ablaze,
to become bombs and destroy culture,
to become poison gas
and consign fellow human beings to oblivion.

At that very moment new life
ready to emerge from the womb
was about to end in silence on its deathbed.

Thus hellish ideas filled the world,
dense black smoke belched up
day and night,
factory workers—male and female,
        faces pale,
were made to work double-time, as if possessed,
and sitting atop the cauldron of hell,
scholars, artists, educators,
politicians
all extolled hellish ideas.

personal
responsibility

Is it not time, people,

to bring back once more

the bright, shining sun

our ancestors praised?

—OCTOBER 1941

The three lines of the third section I deleted from the first edition because I thought that they lacked polish. Labor unions were organized into the Patriotic Production Association; workers, into the Production Warriors; writers, into the Writer's Patriotic Association; politicians too became members of the Imperial Rule Assistance Association and cooperated in the war effort.

New Year's!
A happy time for children and grown-ups alike.
Clothes neat and tidy. Tables laden with holiday food.
Faces lose their stiffness,
necks and shoulders shed their heavy burdens.
Neighbors smile, exchanging greetings,
and promise to get along well this year, too.
In the interval between last year and this,
hearts are so peaceful and gentle—
is this scene a memory of another day?
Or of a time long ago when the gods frolicked
on the bountiful plain of Ashihara?
The authorities use their august powers leniently,
merchants close their shops,
peasants and factory workers, too, celebrate
     the start of new year.
But even as we celebrate,
over the horizon our brothers
stand defenseless before ferocious modern weapons.
When I think of them, my brow clouds, my heart aches.
Ah, when will the world be one
and every last person join in the New Year's feast,
all exchanging affectionate greetings,
     "This year, too, we'll get along well"?
Until that day comes, the sun will be dark.

—JANUARY 1943

RHM: Ashihara (Reed Plain) is one of the epithets for Japan in the myth-
ological sections of the *Kojiki* (A.D. 712) and *Nihongi* (720).

ON A DAY OF POWDERY SNOW

A cold wind blows fiercely; a powdery snow falls.
I go out in search of underwear to buy
and, pleased with myself, return with a quick step.
And then up ahead, a single line approaches
     at a solemn pace,
the man in front carrying a white box chest high.
Did this brave soldier die fighting in the South?
Did he die fighting in the North?
My eyes go hot, tears form, I bow my head
     in a moment of prayer.
The package of underwear is in my hand,
but my pleasure has turned hollow.
A cold wind blows fiercely; a powdery snow falls.

—JANUARY 1943

When Diogenes told the emperor, "Don't stand there—
        you're blocking the sun,"
the sun may well have been just as gentle, warm, and bright
as it is today.
Alexander, clothed in gorgeous imperial robes.
Those in his train, much too long, and Diogenes
        in his ragged robes:
the sun shone just as warmly on them all.
But the one was dead to the sun's touch,
and the other, alive to it.
As I bathe my whole body in the spring sun,
I know how miserable that emperor was.

—FEBRUARY 1943

RIVALRY

From dawn to dusk two creatures of feeling butt heads
until they're both out of breath.
Fierce rivalry: man and woman
deadlocked, unable to back off.
How, finally, do we wind up?
Living as we have until now,
under the same roof.
As if nothing were wrong, day or night, day after day:
how lonely life is
that gives rise to such bitter rivalry!

—MARCH 1943

FEVER

People all have to go through life
at their own body heats.
Aware of what sends my temperature soaring
yet unable to disconnect senses
stretched taut,
I gasp for breath.
100 degrees, 102, 104:
my body heat higher than it has to be, I pant.

THE SILKWORM

Having eaten all it could eat,
the silkworm turned away
even from mulberry leaves fresh off the tree.

Hunched and unmoving,
it reflected on the several molts of its life till then,
and with each day that passed, its head cleared.

As its head cleared,
the silkworm became aware of the many ideas
it had to spin.

DAY AFTER DAY

What a repetition,
simple yet filled with good:
night falls, day breaks.
Day breaks, night falls.
Dusk deepens, the stars shine more brightly,
and people sleep soundly
to wake at dawn
fresh as the very first humans.
I become conscious
of a love welling up inside
that makes me want to call out
      to one and all: "Hello, there!"

        —APRIL 1941

LETTER—TO PETER KROPOTKIN

I have only to write letters
and the universal postal union delivers them
to friends in Taoist China,
to simple Black brothers in far Africa,
to Greenland in the north,
to New York City with its teeming streets.
Ah, you are the veins that connect the world,
delivering letters even to countries at war with each other.
as if unwilling to allow people to go unlinked.
And who's in charge?
Not an American
not a Russian,
but a first beautiful start:
countries consulting,
agreeing, forming a union.
O friends the world over:
let's unite across our length and breadth.
Let's talk, consult, agree, and form a free union;
when we do,
all the things we detest,
all the globe's ills,
will disappear.

—APRIL 1941

Like a katydid with its fine antennae,
I reached out
in search of love,
and like a katydid waving its feelers,
I searched and searched,
but everything I touched was rough and bleak.
Nursing a loneliness only I knew,
I still moved forward.
Then I stopped in utter despair.
I was looking for something
that can't be found.
Yet I refuse
to replace my antennae
with savage, unfeeling horns.
Forever dreaming
a young girl's dreams,
I will raise real children.

—MAY 1941

SPRING GREEN

A May scene: human beings living
where the indigo blue of the sky
meets the spring green of the fields.
The human beings keep breathing
even as the fresh life
germinating in that spring green—
oil paint daubed on thick—
presses in on them;
cut into them with a sharp knife,
and you might draw green blood.
Its silver fuselage glittering today too,
a plane avoids earth's spring green,
virulent green flame burning upward,
and soars so very high into the blue sky.

LET US BE MIDWIVES!

—An untold story of the atomic bombing

Night in the basement of a concrete structure now in ruins.
Victims of the atomic bomb
jammed the room;
it was dark—not even a single candle.
The smell of fresh blood, the stench of death,
     the closeness of sweaty people, the moans.
From out of all that, lo and behold, a voice:
"The baby's coming!"
In that hellish basement, at that very moment,
a young woman had gone into labor.
In the dark, without a single match, what to do?
People forgot their own pains, worried about her.
And then: "I'm a midwife. I'll help with the birth."
The speaker, seriously injured herself,
     had been moaning only moments before.
And so new life was born in the dark of that pit of hell.
And so the midwife died before dawn, still bathed in blood.
Let us be midwives!
Let us be midwives!
Even if we lay down our own lives to do so.

         —SEPTEMBER 1945

This poem appeared first in the inaugural issue of *Chūgoku bunka* (the special issue on the atomic bomb, March 1946). The cellar in the poem was the cellar of the old post office in Senda-machi.

NOT THE SEASON

One day on the sly I planted seeds in my garden.
I waited and waited, but no seedlings appeared.
Finally, I couldn't wait any longer
and dug about on the sly with a hoe,
but I couldn't even find anything that looked like seeds.
I was utterly baffled,
so I asked an old farmer.
"You're asking the impossible, ma'am. It's not the season."
His words struck like a revelation from Heaven.
How stupid I'd been, and now how forlorn.

THE CHILDREN'S VOICES

On a warm winter afternoon
I was tending the vegetable garden.
Absorbed in foolish thoughts, I'd neglected it
      for some time,
and with all the sun we've had this year,
before I knew it, there were weeds.
Normally I tended the garden so religiously, dawn and dusk,
but I'd been too restless and stopped.
Why? I pulled up weeds as I pondered.
"Mommy!" The children were calling, out of breath.
They were home from school.
Ah, how innocent and pure their voices!
From now on, Mommy won't be so silly
as to let weeds grow in our garden.
Our garden won't have a single weed.

—DECEMBER 1945

DO NOT OPEN

In the middle of the night,
strong feelings wake me.
Emotions swirl inside me. Can my small body contain them?
Anger, boundless longing, sighs.
Who was it? Who plunged me into this chaos?
Simple me, quick to trust people—
what do I get back, time after time?
Cold betrayals. People can't live with my sincerity.
Enough!
I'll shut my windows tight.
But right away I begin to long
for a knock.
"Come in!" I say.
People dazzle me
and finally, having stirred my anger, leave.
I think everyone's like me.
You should know better
than to open your windows again. . . .
But how lonely that would be!

—December 1945

RECONSTRUCTION

Insides hollow, windows blown out in the blast,
mouths gaping idiotically,
the great buildings are like people done in
     by the tragedy of the century.
Their trunks a forlorn row, the black trees
     that survived the flames
sing a weird song of death,
and the rubble still holds horror and the stench of death.

To this city—
has time passed so quickly?—
those who fled that day's horrible hell
to villages in the hills return,
recovered in body if not in soul,
and build small huts.

With child, spouse, mother dead,
who needs a large house?
In the small shacks
the survivors call constantly, "Come closer,"
keep each other warm, and carry on.

Day by day, the shacks grow in number, and land
     thought barren—
it too is leveled nicely and soon green with vegetables.
Here and there even now people raise small ridgepoles
     and build houses.

The houses are crude, like those the first humans built
      in the virgin forest,
but these people show even more resolute strength
than the first humans.

—JANUARY 1946

This poem appeared first in the inaugural issue of *Chūgoku bunka*.

Passion!
You always make me do rash things.
And make me fail time and again.
Oh, the hollow loneliness that follows high tension!

But a thirsty heart quickly dreams
of your wonderful embrace.
I ride on your wings, Pegasus coursing the skies,
but always
to emptiness.

Still, I despise
those who never, ever,
have been swept away
in your embrace.
Those people, always calculating,
so ready to stomp
on people you've taken possession of:
are their nights never lonely?

—MARCH 1946

HANDSHAKE

Intent until yesterday on playing war,
the little militarists
throw away their toy weapons and call out:
"Hello, Mr. American Soldier!"

Their small breasts
swell with vague curiosity
about this unknown race:
"Hello, Mr. American Soldier!"

Can it have been you who until yesterday
our fathers were fighting?
"Hello, Mr. American Soldier!"
You open your large mouth, smile cheerfully,
not a bit like the devils
the grown-ups taught us about:
Mr. American Soldier!
We'd like to shake
your large hand.

—FEBRUARY 1946

This poem was deleted in its entirety by prepublication censorship.

OVERGROWN GARDEN

Painfully conscious
of the effort each of us is making,
we piece together our life.
In our feudal garden, crumbling and overgrown,
the only certainty
left
is that we are the children's parents.
Once in a while, something we cannot suppress
lights a brief firefly of love,
and suddenly makes us want to reclaim
what we'd about given up on.
But we quickly lose hope
and retreat into our shells
and the loneliness of separate dreams.

—MARCH 1946

HANDING ON DREAMS

How foolish I was
to focus only
on our love and its problems
and shove you children off to the side!
While Daddy and Mommy
were picking foolishly at each other's love,
just imagine!—
you grew
tall and straight.
Now it's time
for Mommy to hand on to you all her dreams, as is.
Yes, yes, children:
accept Mommy's dreams, as is.
Mind at peace, she'll help you
nurture your dreams.

—MARCH 1946

FATIGUE

Weary of human affection,

I go out back to the vegetable patch.

The little rows of lettuce are as dear to me as sonnets,

and their bright green leaves bring peace

to my tired soul.

Friend, when the fatigue that comes from living

     with emotions too intense

makes me loathe anyone and everyone,

spare me the chatter.

And don't stir up the fire in my heart—

I want to be alone and still.

           —MARCH 1946

THE VOW

We vowed, "Never again,"
but we sink once more into the deep
and, giving malice for malice, exhaust ourselves.
Then, both seeing ourselves in the other,
we take pity
and in due time are back at peace.

If it had been a passing love,
we'd have called it quits long since,
and now we have the children to add
to our vow, "till death do us part."
So even if it seems we always do our best
to break that vow,
you're still my dear companion.
so let's stir the sputtering fire,
take heart, and walk on.
It's not much farther. . . .

—MARCH 1946

PGS
1/3/01

THE VINE

Give me a pole tall and strong,
and I can reach the sky;
I am weak and can't stand on my own,
but by twists and turns,
sending out my tendrils,
I think and I climb.

One stormy night the wind whipped,
and I worried
that it would blow us both down, pole and me,
that the more I clung to it,
the more unreliable it was.
Finally, hoping to work free,
I started to unwind the tendrils of thought
I'd sent twisting and turning for so long.

But dawn did come,
and the sun smiled,
and I realized how fortunate I was
in my pole.

I am a weak vine,
but give me a pole tall and strong,
and I can reach the sky.

TANKA

The China Incident and After

THE DAY OF THE ATOMIC BOMB

In the field out back,
a bluish-white flash;
thinking to myself,
"A flare,"
I look out.

Uneasy about
the weird blue flash,
I step outside—
something
is very wrong.

The sky is
a strange hue—
hazy;
suddenly
it's almost dusk.

Acting on instinct—
air raid!—
I race to our trench,
and hold
my breath.

Crawling out
of the shelter,
I find doors and shoji
blown off
and ceiling down.

Must have been
a near miss,
and the children at school;
I become anxious,
unbearably so.

Go get them!
Rushing out,
I find children
on the street,
coming home crying.

Some
are all bloody;
in my mind's eye
I keep seeing my own children
injured.

They come home,
the older leading
the younger by the hand;
they run to me,
still crying.

Children! Children!
You're alright!
I take them firmly
by the hand
and squeeze hard.

"I'll never let you
out of my sight!"
My love for them

swells
enormously.

A bizarre stormcloud
rising to a peak:
the children are scared
and stay
close by me.

Thunder rolls
like the roar
of a plane;
the children
are terrified.

(The atomic bomb exploded at 8:30 A.M.; by 10:00 A.M. refugees were fleeing to the suburbs in one continuous stream.)

Frightening
street of hell—
each moment
the number of refugees
grows.

The refugees all
have burns;
clothes
are seared
onto skin.

Uninjured
but utterly naked,
a young girl fleeing—

I give her
my child's underpants.

The road to the aid station
outside of town:
the line of refugees
stretches on
and on.

On the relief trucks,
the bodies of the dead
and the injured,
blistered and
horrible.

The last five *tanka* passed prepublication censorship, but I eliminated them from the first edition. On 5 August, the day before the atomic bomb fell, I had been mobilized to clear firebreaks in Tenjin-chō, ground zero. On the morning of 6 August, I saw my husband off to the Mitsubishi Precision Machine factory in Gion where we lived and the two children off to school. Then, as I was cleaning up in the kitchen, I saw the flash. I was four kilometers (two and a half miles) from ground zero.

NIGHTMARE

See tanka version: "Sachiko
Dead in the Atomic Bombing" p. 3
(This is free verse version)

—Going to the aid station to bring home a corpse

After searching more than two days
in vain,
now we learn
the girl
is dead.

Consoling her mother,
we go to retrieve
the girl's corpse:
the city
ravaged by war.

Equipped
for air raid,
we make our way
quickly:
war-ravaged streets.

The last fires
smolder on;
war-gutted streets
still hot
from the flames.

Corpses lie at the roadside,
and the injured form
a great throng:
people
keep aloof.

We near the aid station:
so many ambulances
coming and going
and the stench
of blood.

Near the gate
to the aid station,
it's already awful:
a crowd
of the badly injured.

Lying
every which way,
great numbers
of dead and injured
fill the halls.

In the dim halls
of the aid station,
the living
lie groaning
among the dead.

Among the dead bodies,
a young boy
opens his eyes
and pleads
for water.

He nods gratefully
for a palmful of water:
his mother

surely is
looking for him.

We check
rows of corpses in the halls
one by one,
but can't tell
which one is she.

Not even
their own parents
would know them:
their faces
so utterly transformed.

Dusk falls,
and the halls
with their stench of death
become yet more ghastly,
horrific.

Amid this
horrific reality:
strange
I haven't
stopped breathing.

There, at last—
her corpse;
the injured nearby
lie silent,
eyes open.

Smeared with mud
and black blood,
blistered—
her dear face
gone without a trace.

Loading the corpse
onto the cart we brought,
we leave the aid station;
outside, dusk
closes in.

Carried home
on stretchers and carts—
by parents
and relatives:
so many corpses.

Dusk deepens each moment;
a brightness
over there in the city—
fires
still burning.

(Eerily, the hills around the city were still burning on the
third day.)

Evening falls,
fires on the surrounding hills
gather force,
burn bright red—
without end.

We carry the corpse
from the aid station
through streets
bright with
cremation flames.

I look back at the city:
cremation flames
here and there
dye the black night red—
what sorrow!

The atomic catastrophe occurred on 6 August, and a neighbor girl, a fresh-
man at First Prefectural Girls' Higher School, did not come home. Finally,
on 9 August, we heard that her corpse was in the primary school in Koi, so
three of us—her uncle, her mother, and I—immediately set out at four
o'clock to bring her body home. This is a poem about the scene at the aid
station, the fires still burning as we came home, and the streets bright with
crematory fires. It appeared first in the inaugural issue of *Chūgoku bunka*. I
later composed a free-verse poem about this scene, "Sachiko, Dead in the
Atomic Bombing" (see p. 182).

THE SURRENDER

Compatriots
who had time
only for pride:
now they should reflect
in silence.

"Endure the pain,
and start rebuilding"—
but observer planes
in formation overhead
make me chew my lip.

The huge planes
swoop low:
U.S. insignia
stare me
in the face.

The planes fly
very low overhead,
deafening,
and then
are gone.

"The Surrender" passed prepublication censorship, but I deleted it on my
own from the first edition.

(I)

City of rubble
ravaged by flames:
wind blows
restlessly;
has autumn deepened?

Amid rubble
ravaged by flames,
stand shacks
here and there;
smoke rises.

Shacks with roofs
of burnt tin:
a cold late-autumn shower
wets them
and passes on.

Vermilion
bright as ever,
a fire pumper
lies on its side in a street
ravaged by flames.

Houses
where wives, children, relatives
lived happily:
all now
rubble.

Amid rubble
ravaged by flames,
the last moments
of thousands:
what sadness!

Thousands of people,
tens of thousands:
lost
the instant
the bomb exploded.

Silent, all sorrows
unspoken,
city of rubble
ravaged by flames:
autumn rain falls.

(2)

In a garden
ravaged by flames,
four o'clocks
blossom in silence;
I see no one.

Amid rubble
ravaged by flames,
morning glories bloom,
wet with dew;
yes, winter is near.

Amid rubble
ravaged by flames,

a single blue mustard
leafs out
in such profusion.

The bark of trees
ravaged by flames
is sooty;
branches
send out shoots.

Shacktown
ravaged by flames:
each shack
has its garden,
already green.

(3)

Autumn drizzle stops,
starts again:
winter cold has come
to shacks
ravaged by flames.

Inside,
wood-chip fires burn
brightly, brightly:
families gathered
for supper.

Burned rust-red,
metal pots
roll about;
rays of the setting sun fall
on this city of rubble.

City of rubble
ravaged by flames:
at dusk
I hear cries
from the world of the dead.

City of rubble
ravaged by flames:
walk alone,
and you're
not really alone.

Pine grove
where the wind
once sighed:
only trunks remain,
burned black.

—OCTOBER 1945

Part 1 was composed on the way to Ushita, on the twelfth, and part 2 was composed on the twenty-seventh. Part 3 is set in the pine grove at Izumi Mansion.

NEWSPAPER ARTICLES

Starvation,
homelessness, roadside deaths—
these grim words
run now:
today's newspapers.

Starvation,
homelessness, roadside deaths:
and now
voices are raised
over a poor rice crop.

Starvation,
homelessness, roadside deaths—
one thing after another;
a bitter winter
approaches.

RHM: Wartime censorship kept such "grim words" out of Japan's
newspapers.

Winds roar,
summoning snow;
I'll cleanse my thoughts,
then burrow in
for the winter.

How painful
to be snowed in
for the long winter
and not be done
with such thoughts!

The first snow has fallen;
snowed in
this winter,
I'll aim for
peace of mind.

Snowed in:
this winter
I'll be
especially mindful
of the children.

A crossroad
as dusk falls:
enough already—

I'll stick
to the road I'm on.

I've borne and raised
two children,
but my heart
hasn't lost
the purity of youth.

LANGUAGE

I love
foreign words;
tall, blue-eyed,
my teacher
instructs me.

He speaks Japanese
a bit
too loud:
my tall teacher's
mannerism.

When he speaks,
his words
go straight to my heart;
aren't words
sweet!

The words
my tall teacher
speaks serenely
are childish
but touching.

Our looks
may differ;
but blue-eyed teacher,
you teach us
warmly.

RHM: Shortly after the war ended, Kurihara took English lessons from a
Catholic priest.

LATE AT NIGHT

I've gotten used to waking
in the dead of night to read;
now each night
brings
time I cherish.

The time comes,
and my eyes open
of their own accord;
how peaceful to read
with a clear mind!

A cold coming on?
Pampering myself,
I burrow under the bedding
and read;
night deepens.

The time I don't have
during the day
I have at night;
how I cherish
an uncluttered mind!

I won't disrupt
the family
selfishly;
but I do love
late night reading.

Gradually
sweet sleep descends;
once again
I'm ready
to succumb.

—DECEMBER 1945

SAD TALES FROM DEMOBILIZED SOLDIERS

Wake Island in the south!
Supplies cut off,
so many
starved
to death.

Soldiers coming home
utterly famished
resemble
pathetic
bare trees.

How sad—
men dying
just as they
were about to board
the ship for home.

Mothers who learn
their sons starved to death:
they must weep
every time
they eat.

Wives who learn
their husbands starved to death:
they must weep
every time
they eat.

They say they hunted
frogs and snakes;
the days they lived were
horrible,
nightmarish.

—NOVEMBER 1945

TO A FRIEND, EVACUATED

With three children
she stays in the city—
thinking of her,
my mind
knows no rest.

A letter
reports that she's left:
that's more like it;
but now that she's gone—
desolation.

She said she'd stay
until burned out;
but now, carrying her baby,
she too
has left.

I pity my friend:
to shield her children
from the war,
she's gone to live with
people she hardly knows.

Taking her three children,
she left for the country;
yet every day
I worry
about her.

She left to shield the children
from the war—
friend,
do hold on
through it all.

—July 1945

TOMATO SONGS

In a world
of fierce war,
I grow tomato plants
in the field out back—
at peace.

I said we wouldn't wait
for them to ripen;
but the tomatoes
will be ripe
any day now.

Morning and evening,
I watch my tomato plants
in the field
out back—
and never tire.

Glossy tomatoes
maturing
under the leaves—
a few more days
and they'll be ripe.

The tomatoes in my patch:
fat and round
on the lower branches,
many in clusters
on the upper branches.

One evening
waiting for you
in the field out back,
I pinch off
tomato shoots.

You're here
and keep me company;
we talk of
the ripening tomatoes
in the field out back.

The children too
go check the tomatoes
and report
happily:
they're ripening.

Back at the house,
I wash my hands,
and the soapsuds
turn
green.

LAST EFFECTS

—Seen at the railroad station

Summoned to receive
her dead son's sword,
in front of the station
a mother
breaks down and cries.

Saying, "I'll send it home
to Mother,"
he wrapped it
with his own hands:
she weeps.

The day he wrapped this package,
he was alive
and at his base:
his mother
breaks down and cries.

—JUNE 1945

ELEGY

—At the grave of Mr. Suma

Evil day, the tenth:
the sun is ringed,
and the green
of the new leaves
lacks sparkle.

Cherry blossoms bloom and fall—
that's the rule;
still, I cannot bear
the flames
that consume you.

As the flames
consume you,
even now
I hear
your familiar voice.

When you drank,
you'd grow lively
and speak of your youth—
that I'll never
forget.

Drinking,
you'd talk
more cheerfully yet;
I won't see
that face of yours again.

From childhood,

you were so open-hearted;

with each glass

you became

more so.

—MAY 1945

Mr. Suma was my husband's colleague in the labor section of the company for which he worked and a friend of Mr. Hosoda Tamiki, who kindly wrote the preface to *Kuroi tamago*.

FIRST LETTER

A letter
so long awaited
arrives
New Year's morning—
through the gunfire.

A letter from my brother
came through the battle;
amazing
it made it
all the way!

The brother
we worry about:
he really must be
in good health
and fighting.

The letter he wrote
amid fierce fighting
has arrived;
how thoughtful
he is.

How thoughtful
of Father and Mother!
Amid the gunfire,
he doesn't think
of himself.

—JANUARY 1945

THE BIRTH OF JUNKO

I can't avoid
the pain;
I resolve to bear it,
meet it
head-on.

Heaven and earth
about to split open
and I, too:
then the baby's
first cry.

Having spent all,
all my strength,
I am drowsy,
and then deep sleep
overcomes me.

I close my eyes
but can't sleep—
to think that my baby
lies here
beside me!

She smiles in bliss—
the god of childbirth
must be cuddling her.
I look on
fondly.

People prefer boys,
but I have
no regrets:
Junko, Mariko,
my jewels.

My second daughter Junko was born in 1939. That night there was a long procession of people carrying lanterns; they were celebrating the capture of Hangzhou.

NEW-SOLDIER BROTHER

We have come so far,
across mountains and rivers,
and the thundering sea
comes
into view.

High waves
attack the beach
again and again—
we watch,
avidly.

Beyond the platform,
a hill not far off,
its grass winter-dead:
we are here—
Hamada.

Iwami Hamada
of the high waves:
powdery snow
swirls
in the pounding wind.

Iwami Hamada
of the high waves:
the barracks
by the hill—
that's where you are.

Warriors in the thousands,
you among them:
New-Soldier Brother
how are you
getting on?

(In the visiting room)

Dear brother,
in attractive
new uniform;
it almost
becomes you.

New-Soldier Brother
so dear to me;
you greet us
with
a salute.

You've become
a fine soldier;
but looking you up
and down,
I'm sad.

Wanting to give you
all kinds of things to eat,
I unwrap
what we've brought
in the crowded visiting room.

New-Soldier Brother:
we crowd around you
and urge on you
fruit
and candy.

Around each soldier
crowd his relatives;
they exchange
joys and sorrows,
never running out.

A soldier's young wife,
a baby in her arms:
it's crowded,
so she hides
her feelings.

A rare, brief
time together:
with many people about
she seems
to hold back.

The child
doesn't know the rules
for soldiers:
"Daddy, come home with us!"
He can't stop crying.

———————

New-Soldier Brother
we leave you
and come home;
how we long
for Iwami Hamada.

—JANUARY 1944

In January 1944 my younger brother reported for duty to the regiment at Hamada in Shimane Prefecture. Just before the regiment was sent to the front in China, my father, my husband, and I traveled there together to bid him goodbye.

MISCELLANY

Seen at an angle,
momentarily,
goldfish in a crystal bowl:
they swim
in stately fashion.

Brocade carp
more than a foot long:
they look heavy
and swim
sedately.

The buds
of the persimmon trees
ringing my parents' home:
how they glisten
in the sun!

Persimmons buds
aren't as showy
as the full blossoms,
but they glisten—
so beautiful!

The blossoms
of the lily magnolia
come into heavy bloom;
all the other trees
have new leaves.

The blossoms
of the lily magnolia—
so voluptuous;
heavy and
reddish purple.

He says he sees
only something red,
and that but faintly:
the blind young man
seems so forlorn.

All the things I see
effortlessly—
do I
really see colors
and shapes?

To see for a time,
he'd give up
ten years of his life
without
thinking twice.

In red cotton shoes,
my daughter
takes her first steps,
her feet
unsteady.

My husband and I
don't talk much
any more;

we communicate
via the children.

I wasn't going to speak,
but I couldn't help myself
and burst out,
"Will you look
at our children!"

In early spring
where the weak sun
warms the sidewalk,
I make chalk drawings
with the children.

The children's drawings,
so childlike,
are precious;
I can't
step on them.

I didn't notice
the children had left,
but the chalk drawings
are still here—
lots of them.

LOVE OF SELF

The feathery down
of baby birds
is so soft—
oh, to press it
to my heart.

Those the world calls
good mothers, good wives:
most
have hearts
that are empty.

Those the world calls
good mothers, good wives:
occasionally
they must want to let go
of the selves they hold to.

Discarding
what is true for me,
becoming empty like them:
I don't know
how.

I'm the mother of two;
but most of the time
I think
only
of myself.

I feel for
children with such a mother;
when I embrace them,
my love becomes
stronger still.

He denounced
what England did,
but—bald-faced liar—
he'll do
the same.

Individuals attack,
and it's a crime;
nations attack
and win
praise.

Have-not Germany
attacks have nations,
and almost everyone
voices
support.

Invoking the class struggle,
have-not nations
wage war
against
the haves.

Ludicrous:
spouting anti-Communism,
allied countries
challenge
the haves.

Right and wrong
aren't the issue;
his great speed
in all directions
earns him praise.

Hitler:
gain beckons,
and the base person discards
what he himself
trumpeted.

"Anti-Communism
and the Non-Aggression Treaty—
no contradiction":
poor Hitler—his tongue
confuses me.

To save the treasures
of the heritage:
in the end, alas!
Paris
surrenders.

What's so great about
Hitler's Blitzkrieg?
Avid for blood,
he goes
on the attack.

Hitler takes small nations
one after the other
and swells with pride;
many people
applaud him.

—JUNE 1940

All eleven stanzas were deleted in prepublication censorship.

RESPECT FOR HUMANITY

They denounced us
for being
too materialistic;
but what of their
"human resources"?

"It's state policy,
so have children!"
Sounds as easy as
getting hens
to lay more eggs.

"It's state policy,
so have children!"
In the end,
respect for life
gets trampled.

Goods for consumption
twenty years later—
women, get angry
at systematized
life and death!

Militarism
is an abomination;
women of the world—
until it dies,
don't have children!

The old soldier, too,
beaten
with a horse whip
for not
saluting.

In 1941 the Ministry of Public Welfare established a wartime population policy, based on Nazi ideas of eugenics, prohibiting contraception and abortion; in the postwar era of shortages of housing and food, it lifted the prohibition on abortion. This is the basis of the current Eugenics Protection Act. The movement to "amend" the Eugenics Protection Act that has recently [1983] become controversial can be described as aiming at a reversion to the prewar system.

MEMORIES

Were he still alive,
I'd say nothing about him;
learning that he's dead
awakens
memories.

It's a full ten years
in the past;
suddenly
it all comes
back to me.

The pattern of his kimono
as we talked
in the shade
of the cosmos flower:
I can see it now.

His letters came,
beautiful in form
and in content—
I couldn't
contain myself.

When his spirits were high,
he'd stick his chest out:
I can see
that habit of his
even now.

We wrote poems
back and forth:
memories
from my
brief girlhood.

RHM: Kurihara wrote this *tanka* sequence on learning of the death of a
contemporary of hers, a composer of *tanka* to whom she had grown close.

PADDY FIELD

When the wind blows,
it turns the surface
of the paddy
into hundreds, thousands
of ripples.

The dark gray surface
of the paddy:
in the evening light,
scattered frogs
begin to croak.

The mountain over there
rises upright,
trailing lowlands about it;
over the farther mountains,
rain clouds form.

The rainy-season sky
seems suddenly
about to clear,
but a fine mist
falls instead.

In the rainy season
sometimes the sky lightens,
and the rain pauses,
only to pour
once more.

POLLINATED BY THE WIND

Did spring snow fall
while we weren't looking?
Early rice
already
in bloom.

The autumn wind
sighs,
and the white blossoms
on rice stalks
mingle.

The wind blows;
the rice plants
nod to each other
and, heads touching,
mingle in the wind.

Ah, starry host
on autumn nights—
more brilliant
than
the full moon.

Big Dipper—
who set it there?
Ah, autumn night,
the earth wet
and sparkling.

As I toss and turn,
my ice pack
sloshes:
so lonely, this night
when crickets cry.

RECORD OF MY PASSION

After months when passion
doesn't burn
inside me,
suddenly
I'm desolate.

Time passes,
and I'm not on fire,
all's well?
Suddenly
I'm desolate.

I've wanted
not to feign love,
but it's been months;
at the thought,
I'm desolate.

Can I make do
with feigned love?
Don't envy
those who put up
a front!

The man desires,
the woman feigns,
and they make do—
shallow
happiness!

How desolate
I am:
unless I stop reasoning,
I can't
feel.

I lie right beside him
in bed;
but reason keeps me
from being swept away—
desolation.

I'm not
wood or stone;
I'd give my life
to burn
with honest love.

Children asleep at my side:
Mother will never
sacrifice you
to her
inner conflict.

I'll smash
this heart of mine;
for their sake
I'll sacrifice
myself.

I've thought it through,
decided,
and alas!

I'm no better
than those I scorn.

Unselfconscious,
I know peace;
self-conscious,
I suffer—
all the sadder!

LOVE

You're enraptured by what you've got; but know that
    treason breeds in your embrace.
A vow is a vow, to be sure; but don't forget
    to win it day by day.
A woman of many dreams would drag you into her dreams;
    but we simply can't share rapture, so she is desolate.
Was the thought of him lurking deep in my subconscious?
    I dreamed of him and shivered.
I deny that such things happen, but I saw his face
    in a dream.
A fine lens, and suddenly a face appears:
    that's how consciousness works.

RHM: Despite its inclusion among the *tanka*, this poem is not a *tanka*. In its modulation from the first theme (lines 1–3, husband) to the second theme (lines 4–6, another man), it resembles *tanka*, but in form it is free verse. However, in length of line and in the almost complete absence of punctuation, it differs from the author's other free verse.

MY FRIEND GIVES BIRTH TO A SON

I touch him—
a life so fragile
it may melt
like light snow:
newborn baby.

My hands holding him
are large and coarse;
so soon after birth,
he is pure,
unsullied.

I hold him:
the gentle touch
of his hands
on my breast—
how sweet!

The world is so harsh
that I said no more babies;
my resolve
begins to
weaken.

Holding my friend's child,
I yield for a while
to rapture—
a mother's
emotions.

—1940

FATHER, MOTHER

Mother's dear hands,
rough and tough
from tilling the fields:
tears well up
in my eyes.

Father and Mother
intent to distraction
on raising me:
I think of them
even now.

The hair
at her temples
already white:
I think of Mother,
and the tears spill down.

Parents worry about children;
children, about parents:
ah, this world in which
they must go
their separate ways.

I call them
Father, Mother, Brother, Sister,
yet they don't know
the sorrows
of my life.

ANESTHETIC INJECTION

—At the dentist's

The dentist says,
"Easy, now. Relax."
But involuntarily
I become tense
and breathe shallow breaths.

The moment I think
the shot is over,
I inhale
and exhale
raggedly.

My breathing sped up,
but now it slows down—
my nerve
must have gone
numb.

The shot has taken
full effect;
slowly, slowly,
I
go under.

CACTUS FLOWERS

Blossoming in among
the spines of the cactus,
the large white flowers
seem to glow
from within.

Pure
as a maiden,
the large white flowers
of the cactus:
don't touch!

It must be tough,
blooming in this world;
in the evening
the large white petals
fold back up.

(Air-raid drill)

Lights on earth
are all out;
see how tonight's stars
sparkle
so brightly.

Countless sparkling stars—
each one
follows its own
solemn
and solitary path.

The path you take
and the path I take—
each path solitary,
permanent,
narrow.

KOREAN MAIDEN

Korean maiden,
lovely and chaste
in casual gown:
with
long black hair.

Maiden with black hair
long, plaited,
and bound up
with red cloth:
her black hair.

Korean maiden,
skin so fine,
lightly
powdered:
dazzling.

Like the celestial maidens
who strolled the skies,
Korean maiden
strolls the city street,
relaxed.

Korean maiden
with simple beauty
and clear gaze:
so
lovely.

TO A FRIEND

Day three and day four
I get through calmly;
after day seven,
I see only
her face.

My friend's smile—
it alone
clings to my mind's eye
and won't leave
and won't go.

Thinking of her
makes me eager to meet:
like the loves
I knew
as a girl.

There's a break
in the long rain,
and I go out:
the road is muddy,
but I don't mind.

Born female,
you and I
swap the griefs
that are woman's lot:
ah, what contentment!

On the street corner,
you and I
swap talk
of our children,
smile and part.

WAKING FROM A NAP

I wake lazily
from a nap;
my mind is
utterly vacant,
like an imbecile's.

The empty feeling
on waking from a nap:
I try
to gather myself
but can't.

I'm lazy and can't get up
right away:
I wake from a nap,
and reality
is so lonely.

———————

Thunder rumbles afar off;
the sky's blue
grows deeper,
and the sun
sparkles.

Thunder rumbles
from the white edges
of fleecy clouds,
even though the sun
is shining.

ELEGY

—For Ms. Ōhara Rinko

She kept the wishy-washy
at arm's length,
she who yearned so
for the ardent
and fiery.

In this world of ours,
people like her
are hard to find anywhere;
I hope to find her
in my dreams.

I thought of her now,
just now;
yet I've learned
she died
long, long ago.

I'd cross mountains
and rivers
in search of her—
Ōhara Rinko,
where is she?

I think of you,
angel riding
through the skies,
living now
a shining new life.

—1941

FOR MS. TAKEMOTO KIKUYO

I speak,
but your face shows no sign;
you can't hear,
and your face
is painful to look at.

When I speak,
and someone interprets,
finally you nod,
"Yes, yes"—
how moving.

I won't speak
of trivial things;
your effort leaning forward
trying so to hear—
how moving.

My words seem
to get through at last,
and after a bit
you do smile—
how moving.

———————

My hand on the forehead
of the sleeping child,
too sick to know

day from night—
I sigh with sorrow.

The child doesn't ask
for a thing,
merely sleeps quietly—
I keep watch,
helpless.

How moving:
this child beyond the help
of parents
fights the disease
on her own.

It's so lovely
when the trees on the low hills
put forth
tender buds,
each tree different.

How touching:
trunks straight and bare,
the young trees
whose names I don't know
put forth buds.

Trees whose pink-tipped buds
are still hard
stand among
trees
fully in bud.

The trees are
covered in silver;
their buds
have
white fuzz.

The cherries low on the hills
are in bloom;
giant trees farther up
are still dark,
no buds yet.

Blooming on each branch
as if to bend it,
the double-blossomed cherries—
translucent
in the noonday sun.

The single-blossomed cherries
fall and blow away:
the double-blossomed cherries
now begin
to bloom gorgeously.

Reaching the high field
where upper branches
bloom so green,
I hear
a warbler.

———————

At my old home,
only winter-wither;
in the high field over there,
the sun
breaks through.

The high fields
are in bright sunshine;
tying mountain to mountain,
a rainbow
paints an arc.

—1940

Afterword

EVEN AFTER the U.S.-Japan peace treaty went into effect and Japan regained its independence, Occupation censorship cast a long shadow in the form of the aftereffects of the atomic taboo. In the case of "atomic bomb literature," people continued to smile coldly and ask, "Does such a genre—'atomic bomb literature'—really exist?" Writers and poets who had experienced the bomb suffered from the psychological pressure of censorship and from alienation inside and outside the literary establishment, and after hard and bitter struggles, they died sad deaths.

Hara Tamiki committed suicide. Tōge Sankichi damaged his lungs through overwork and died during an operation to remove a lung. Ōta Yōko died suddenly on a trip, her death the last of many setbacks. Shōda Shinoe died a terrible death: breast cancer brought on by radiation sickness.

Works that came to grips with the atomic bomb were not included in anthologies and for a long time, into the 1970s, were not accorded citizenship in the realm of postwar literature.

Still, in today's nuclear age when the existence of nuclear weapons continues to threaten all human beings, atomic bomb literature has come to be regarded as something that should not be shied away from, a theme common to the whole world.

Last summer the works of Ōta Yōko were published in four volumes (Tokyo: Sanichi, 1982), and this summer the fifteen-volume *Nihon no genbaku bungaku* [Atomic bomb literature of Japan] (Tokyo: Horupu) and the Ōe Kenzaburō/

Japan P.E.N. Club volume *Nihon no genbaku bungaku besuto 10* [Atomic literature of Japan: the best ten] will appear.

As if leading the way for this great movement, Shōda Shinoe's book of poems, *Sange* [Flowers for the dead], was reissued this February in a limited edition by Tsukio Sugeko of *Tanka shijō* [Best tanka].

Sange is a book of poems to console those mourning relatives lost in the atomic bomb. Because it was absolutely impossible to publish this volume as long as Occupation censorship was in force, the late Shōda Shinoe resolved to publish it clandestinely; shaking off the advice of those around her not to, that if she were found out, MacArthur would sentence her to death, she ran off a mimeographed edition of 150 copies.

Following on *Sange* and commemorating the thirtieth anniversary of Tōge Sankichi's death, the commemoration committee republished three of his works in May. These works included the mimeographed version of *Genbaku shishū* [Poems of the atomic bomb] that Tōge published during the Korean war; he dedicated five hundred of them to the Great Peace Festival in Hiroshima.

Kuroi tamago follows on those volumes. *Kuroi tamago* (1946), *Sange* (1947), and *Genbaku shishū* (1951) were all reprinted or republished in the thirty-eighth year after the war: this fact indicates a common determination, in today's crisis, to authenticate the meaning of that time.

There was a time when one could not mention atomic bomb literature without encountering resistance; today, we speak of it without a second thought. We must not forget that it was the hard and bitter struggles during the Occupation of the survivor-writers and survivor-poets who are now dead that brought about this situation.

As this volume appears, I cannot help thinking of the fate of poetry. Poems are the manifestation of the spirit at its most free, so poets experience coercion at the hands of the powers that be, and their poetry is suppressed. Before and during the war, so very many poets were coerced and jailed by the regular police and the special police, were forced to throw down their pens, grew accustomed to censorship, or had their pens twisted against their will to protect themselves! How much censored or suppressed poetry do we still not know about even now? The same conditions held for poets in the era of the Occupation and the Korean War.

If we extend our gaze abroad, we see that poets live under the same conditions. In many countries of the Third World, in particular, poets who stand in the vanguard of the masses demanding democracy and human rights are the first objects of state coercion.

Kuroi tamago is being reprinted after thirty-seven years and is seeing the light of day in complete form for the first time. I am fully aware that its fate is linked with the fate of those many other books of poems of resistance.

Moreover, I realize that the publication of this book enjoys the support of all the many people who will not allow a new prewar era to come to pass, who long for peace. . . .

—JUNE 1983

PART TWO

SELECTED LATER POEMS

THE POET

I'LL ALWAYS KEEP SINGING

Despite everything, I'll keep singing.
Bald pates shining,
the unrighteous swagger about,
fill the air with the smell of rot,
raise raucous voices: amid the din,
with all my might
I'll keep singing, No, no, no.

They set up a vulgar altar,
they nurture the spirit of the herd,
thunderous applause fills the plaza;
amid it all, alone, I'll keep singing
a song of negation.
No. No. No. No.
I'll sing it a thousand times, ten thousand times.

The night's still dark.
I can't sing lovely songs
of morning flowers,
bright sun,
green of the plants,
but tomorrow will surely come.
In the darkness that smells of the rising tide
I'll speak
to you, dear friend,
and when it has grown light
about us,
I'll make sure it's you.

The night's still dark.
Shut up within the walls of night,
walls that yield not at all,
I'll always keep singing.

—JULY 1952

I BEAR WITNESS FOR HIROSHIMA

As a survivor, I wish first of all
to be a human being,
and all the more, as one mother,
I would weep over them now, while they are alive,
the tears I'd shed over their corpses
should the clear skies above these red-cheeked infants
and everyone else
suddenly one day rip open
and condemn many to be burned alive.
Above all, I oppose war,
and even if they try under one label or another to punish
a mother's saying no to her children's death,
I will not flee or hide,
for that day's hell
is seared onto my retinas.

August sixth, 1945:
the sun rose, and soon
people set gravely about their daily rounds;
suddenly
the city was blown away,
skin blistered,
the seven rivers filled with corpses.

The tale goes
that if those who get a look at hell talk of hell,
hell's devil-king will call them back,
but as a survivor, witness for Hiroshima,
I testify wherever I go,
and even if it should cost me my life, I sing,
"An end to war!"

—September 1952

LOST SUMMER

A chilly gem of a morning,
a bunch of grapes, translucent blue,
left unpicked.
Even the sand that all summer long had broiled,
roasted, and boiled
is now suddenly quiet and compacted.
Nothing burns;
the seasons have their rhythm,
so everything sinks back into coolness.

The summer sky that burned so,
the sand glittering as if about to explode.
Since the summer of 1945,
our summers have surged up
and then boiled over.
We loved each other
and always called gently to each other.
Your blood gone thin,
you laid your hand atop mine:
"You know, my hands really are cold."
But
in the eighteenth summer
it was as if you had got lost, a yellow butterfly
off among thunderclouds—
only an echo came back to me.
The summer that glittered down on us has departed,
and the sand that shimmered like white gossamer
in the sunlight is absolutely still once again.

It burns no longer.
It does not boil;
inorganic and cool,
it is simply a grainy layer.

—SEPTEMBER 1963

BEACHED

Absolutely empty, this white beach
washed by the great waves,
except for me, tossed up.

The rays of the sun sizzle
through my thin scales,
and sting like arrows.
And the broiling sand of the beach
burns my belly
as if to set even my innards boiling.

Those who were with me—
where did they go?
Together we might have ridden the great waves
that came surging majestically in;
instead, they threw me up onto the beach
along with the great waves
and, riding the waves, went out again.

I'd dreamed of lining up with them
and riding the great waves.
As for them, after the great waves raged,
the brine became more bitter,
but they lost all sense for the bitterness of the brine
and are probably swimming,
through forests of trembling seaweed,
scales sparkling
like cheap jewelry.

I'm high and dry, but I won't die.
For I have the boundless sea.

Summoning my last bit of strength,
I leap from beach to sea.
For a while I'll gasp for breath,
slowly filtering
the bitter brine
through my dark red gills.
But then I'll bend and stretch
my steel backbone, free,
and with supple sinews and slender fins
swim the rough seas, free.

The crafty waves are elusive—
try to grab them
and they slip away,
but I dream that the day I ride them
will surely come.

—DECEMBER 1964

PGS 1/3/01

Many, many days of sunshine,
many, many days of clouds—
I've lived quite a long life already
and grieved, rejoiced,
suffered
as many times.
In that time people I loved
disappeared suddenly from my side.
You were the first taken from me.
What great happiness you brought us,
first-time parents, destitute though we were!
As your second birthday approached,
you finally started to babble;
were you alive today,
you'd already be a young father,
but you remain always the baby you were then.
Next my younger brother and older sister died young,
        one after the other;
how Mother, as old then as I am now,
must have suffered!
Over long years my husband's father, mother,
        older sister too
died one after the other,
and with each death
we cremated loved ones.
So many times now we've wept and then,
when our tears finally dried, choked on new tears.

Early this year I lost my aged mother.
Up until a few minutes before the end,

Mother was talking quietly:
that's how her gentle life came to a close.
Death is the end of life,
not the end of love.

Ten fingers aren't enough to count
relatives, friends, and the many loved ones
now lost from memory
whom I've buried.
When I think of them,
there are times now
when death seems almost a friend.
May those who are alive be happy
and those who are dead rest in peace—
as if life and death are continuous,
loved ones seem now
to be calling me.

Since the day I was born,
many, many long days of sunshine,
many, many days of clouds.
Until the day I die,
how many days of sunshine will there be?
How many days of clouds?

—JANUARY 1965

WORDS—COME BACK TO LIFE!

Words—have they no power
to bubble up from the grass roots,
make groves and forests tremble,
lay siege to the castles of the arrogant?
The words born glistening
out of that burnt-out waste where the dead sleep—
have they died?

Shedding the same blood
that flows on the battlefield,
the young try today to grab hold of their tomorrows,
their day-after-tomorrows, their eternal tomorrows.
Hemmed in by nightsticks, smeared with blood,
the young fly head over heels
off the bridges.

Freezing cold night:
embracing darkness
so dark that even the flames shooting skyward
from the person who set himself afire—
as if the girl selling matches had lit them all—
cannot brighten it,
the lords of the arrogant castles
set out for nuclear hell.

Dead words, come back to life!
Bathed in the blood of the young,
lighted by the flames of the man who set himself afire,
the song of the dead, song without words,
calls out.

—OCTOBER 1968

WORDS DIED

She was sick and in bed.
The sound of feet going up and down the stairs
reached her ears many, many times,
but no one came to where she was.
In that house, a long time before,
words had died.
Words became commands and reports, nothing more,
and even those came to an end;
everyone left the house silent
and returned silent.
A deep, uncrossable pool formed,
and she was up to her neck
in that pool
of tears
from thousands of years of women crying.
When she dies,
the pool may utter words at last.
While she lives, even the words about to issue
        from her throat
hold back,
for only grudges can grow
in the deep silence.
When she dies
words may come to life again,
but as long as she lives
words are dead.
Yet she goes on living
her cruel life.

—DECEMBER 1969

FROZEN EYES

Under smog-filled skies
in the city,
the temperature suddenly dropped
and everyone froze
hard as frozen fish.
Frozen lips stopped uttering;
tongues turned rigid.
If, unable to bear it,
you summoned all your strength
and spoke of love,
instantly the words became malicious blocks of ice
thrown back in your face.
As the temperature fell farther and farther
only the veins
inside frozen people remained active,
barely circulating
red liquid.
These blocks of ice won't melt
in a thousand years.
When frozen people
die,
frozen eyes
spill hot tears.
But even the hot tears of the dying
can't thaw
the thousand-year freeze.

—MAY 1973

LEAVES BLOWING IN THE WIND

Standing on the corner passing out leaflets,
I appealed to people.
Leaves blowing in the wind,
my words fell on deaf ears.
Words, words, words:
I said them over and over,
but they failed to move people.

I stood on the corner
like a tree
and repeated words
as useless as windblown leaves,
and my words failed to move
housewives with their shopping baskets.
"Words mean less to me than the price of carrots."
Young mothers went by,
pushing carriages carrying babies decked out beautifully,
just like dolls,
but my words couldn't even get past the carriages.
Words, words, words:
I wanted them to have force and meaning,
but I couldn't help doubting their power.
I had fallen under the spell of words,
I had fallen into the snare of words.
Words had become windblown leaves
and threatened to bury me.
What were they to me,
the people I encountered on the corner?
What drove me to stand on the corner?
The rumbling of tanks drew near—

I could all but hear it,
marching boots echoed—
I could all but hear them,
yet the people in the street wore bright colors,
seemed happy, and chattered away.

—September 1973

EXPOSURE

I wear blue, like a prison uniform.
A woman in white asks me to open wide
and, as if feeding livestock,
shoves white medicine from a tube down my throat.

I press my chest
to an upright white stand,
and the x-ray camera
clicks.
Radiation passes through my body.

The white stand falls forward,
and now, face down,
I'm told
to hold my breath and lie on my right side,
on my left, on my back.
I obey, and each time the x-ray camera clicks
and radiation passes through my body.

I wonder how much of the radiation
I received with the flash and blast that summer
is still inside me.
Is its half-life over?
Black forebodings flit across my mind:
damaged genes, chromosomes,
children with congenital defects.

The white stand returns to upright,
and I'm back where I began.
I turn to the right,

and in front of me is another white stand.
As if in an oil press,
I'm squeezed and squashed
from front and back.
Under the eye of a video camera,
I drink white fluid, a sort of sludge,
from a large cup.

Holding my breath,
I turn left, turn right.
Each time the machine clicks,
and radiation passes through my body.

The data:
is it entered
into the ABCC's computer
and sent to the United States?
The ABCC continues even now
to pursue *hibakusha;*
from atop the hill,
it overlooks all the hospitals in the city.

—DECEMBER 1977

IN MEMORIAM

—Looking back on my husband's life

Come back, happy memories!
Come back, days of good health!
The days you were critically ill,
so filled with pain and bitterness,
so filled with sadness.

Come back, memories of your stalwart youth!
You believed in, planned for Kropotkin's society
      without power—
society of free thinking and free agreement.
Even up against the wall, you prayed to no god;
young hero, you made the impossible possible.

When the China Incident began,
you were drafted, sent onto a hospital ship.
What things you witnessed
on shore leave in Shanghai!
You preached the immorality of the war—
"I saw what I saw"—
and were court-martialed.

Under the Occupation army's press code,
you published the issue on the atomic bomb
and were summoned before the CIC;
accusing your accusers,
you charged American democracy was a fraud.
In the postwar land reform,
you fought to uphold the rights of tenant farmers;
on school consolidation,

you argued
against impersonal education in large schools,
fought on the side of the residents,
and kept the elementary school here.

The morning of the march to the City Council,
the police were waiting for the chance
     to crack down, and you called out,
"Hey, Chief! We're headed for the City Council
to exercise our right of petition. In the interests
     of public safety,
please stop the cars!
I request it as a member of the legislature."
Guided by police,
the demonstration set out.

In retaliation for his stand against school consolidation
the principal was demoted,
and teachers union and residents joined forces again,
     fought,
and won in the Supreme Court.
Fighting to democratize the Ōta River fishing cooperative,
ensuring the land beyond the levee would go to the tillers,
you sought to build a world
where truth prevails
even if its voice is that of an eighty-year-old grandma.
You fought all your life
for people's rights, for human rights.

On August sixth, thirty-five years ago
236 volunteer brigaders from Mitsubishi Precision's
     Gion plant
were mobilized to clear firebreaks

in Koami-chō, eight hundred meters from ground zero,
and beneath the mushroom cloud they were burned black.
With the relief squad, you rushed to the scene
and on the way—in Yokogawa—were struck
    by black rain;
your shirt got as dirty
as if dipped in coal tar.
You housed the victims of the bomb
in the company dorm and the school,
nursed them day and night,
and cremated the dead on the playground.
In September pink dots appeared all over your body,
    and you hemorrhaged,
ran a high fever, hallucinated,
your mind wandering in atomic deserts.

Radioactivity
slowly ate away at you from within.
We'd forgotten it many years later
when suddenly it appeared—the cruelty of the atomic bomb;
the authorities said the cause wasn't clear
and refused to accept responsibility.
Though thirty-five years have passed
and the state still hasn't compensated them
    for its war guilt.
Hibakusha die, one after the other.

The blood of the three million that flowed
at home and abroad, from the Aleutians
    to far Nomonhan,
gave birth to a peace constitution that renounces war.
The constitution gives meaning to the deaths
    of those who died

and ensures that children will have a future.

After the war you fought the good fight

for the constitution, against nukes, against war.

Rest in peace.

To prevent the mistake from being repeated,

we will keep your fight alive,

create a large, strong groundswell,

and build a future without war.

From your distant abode,

watch over our struggle.

—OCTOBER 1980

RHM: Kurihara writes CIC, which in "*Kuroi tamago* to watakushi," 120–21, she translates as *minkan jōhōbu*, "civil intelligence section," but CIC does not appear in the organizational charts of the Occupation. Article 9 of Japan's postwar constitution (a document drafted by General MacArthur's staff) reads: "the Japanese people forever renounce war as a sovereign right of the nation. . . . In order to accomplish the preceding paragraph, land, sea, and air forces, as well as other war potential, will never be maintained. The right of belligerency of the state will not be recognized."

THE GILDED HEARSE

In the garden out front,
people in black stand around,
waiting for the gilded hearse to depart.
Who can it be
in the gilt shrine
carved with birds and flowers
and mounted on wheels?
At this last parting,
people sob
as they cover the deceased with flowers.
The day is not far off when I too
will depart in that gilded hearse.
The day comes when its metal doors will close on me
and I'll depart this world forever.
Until that day
I want to blow my flute
and sing
for the sake of those alive today
and the children of the future:
"Don't turn this globe into ruins!"

—JUNE 1988

LIFE AND DEATH

—Mourning Nagaoka Hiroyoshi

Riding the wind,
you danced up into the sky.
Lately, longing for your native place,
you'd spoken with birds and insects
and written a poem of love for your cat Osei,
and in your soft voice you sent me
a signal, "Sayonara,"
but I didn't catch on.

Hara Tamiki fell from the sky;
you danced up into the sky—
neither of you could join in this world's corruption.
You saw yourselves
with no role in this world,
so you departed.

Is the wind you?
Does the wind encircle you? You said
the wind always
blows away the finer ones.

At the end you weighed only eighty pounds,
the winds encircled you,
and suddenly you danced up into the sky.

I who am old but still alive—
what of me?
My firstborn son died at two,
my brother and sister died young,

as time passed, father, mother, husband, sister
all died.
I who survive:
have I come this far at the cost of my relatives?
Have I grown old
at the cost of those dear to me?

I, made of coarser stuff—
I didn't fall from the sky,
I don't rise up into the sky.
I have to crawl along the ground.
And I have to see
what those who could not bear to live
could not bear to see.

—SEPTEMBER 1989

Hara Tamiki was the author of *Summer Flowers*.

RHM: For a translation of *Summer Flowers*, see Richard H. Minear, ed. and trans., *Hiroshima: Three Witnesses* (Princeton: Princeton University Press, 1990), 41–113. Nagaoka Hiroyoshi (1932–89) was author of *Genbaku bunken o yomu* [Reading atomic bomb literature, 1982] and other books; he committed suicide on 14 August 1989.

HIROSHIMA

SACHIKO, DEAD IN THE ATOMIC BOMBING

Iwojima fell,
Okinawa fought to the last man—
not even empty funerary urns came back,
cities throughout the land were burned to blackened waste,
and then
August sixth, 1945:
blue sky perfectly still.
Air-raid hood of padded cotton
over your shoulder,
you were mobilized to raze buildings
      for the forced evacuations—

suddenly,
the blue flash:
buildings collapse,
fires blaze,
and amid swirling smoke
hordes of people in flight
thread their way through downed wires.

On the evening of the third day
we brought your corpse home.
A dark night: air-raid alarm
that was never lifted.
In the black night Hiroshima burned red.
The eve of the surrender,
all Japan as if holding vigil.
A dark room sealed off by blackout curtains.
You laid out before the *butsudan*,
a white handkerchief over your face.

In the dusk at the aid station

crazed victims

had shouted like wild animals

and raced about the classrooms;

grotesquely swollen, people with burns had groaned

and given off alive the stench of death.

The corpses were lined up like so many heaps of rags

on the dirt floor of Koi Primary School,

and we knew you only by your metal ID.

Over your face—

a white handkerchief

someone had placed there.

The handkerchief was stuck fast to your burns

and would not come off.

A junior in girls' higher school,

not understanding what the war was about,

you died, Sachiko, before you could blossom.

Your mother

draped a brand-new gown,

white and flowered,

over the school uniform burned to tatters

and seared onto your skin.

"I made it for you, but because of the war,

you never got to wear it."

Her arms around you, she broke down and wept.

—AUGUST 1946

RHM: A *butsudan* is a Buddhist altar in a private home. Koi was then a suburb of Hiroshima, at the foot of the hills immediately to the west of the city. This free-verse poem repeats the story of the *tanka* sequence "Nightmare" in *Kuroi tamago*. See Kurihara's note to that poem.

p. 86-90
tanka,
version

CITY UNDER GROUND

Like a keloid hand opened out,
seven rivers flow, full of the water of agony.
Under the city in the delta,
the burned corpses of August still lie, tightly compacted.
Now, as then, roasted by broiling sand and sun,
now, as then, fallen in heaps in burning streetcars,
now, as then, burned hands holding tight to burned hands,
now, as then, heaped like trash on the concrete floor
    of a dark aid station,
now, as then, pinned beneath heavy beams—
not yet humus,
they form instead
a mushy human mud.

Finally covered over, the city under ground
will become a layer of rubble and bones,
the twentieth century's
atomic stratum.
It will bring a gleam to the eyes
of archeologists—
"Hiroshima: that was a civilization!"

—August 1952

Hiroshima: nothing, nothing—
old and young burned to death,
city blown away,
socket without an eyeball.
White bones scattered over reddish rubble;
above, sun burning down:
city of ruins, still as death.
Look: on my sleeve, my shoulder,
covering every last inch—
yes, a swarm of black flies!
Bred in the pulpy entrails and putrid flesh
of our dead,
white larvae grow fat on bloody pus,
cling to the rubble.
Shoo, fly! Shoo, fly! But they don't shoo.
They swarm over clothes, attached almost.

Seven years have passed, and even today the flies
buzz all over, spreading invisible bacteria.
The busy square in front of the station.
Wearing khaki, the Police Reserve is everywhere;
the smell of leather is strong.

Ever since being hit that day
by a blast fierce enough to blow away the globe,
this city has lost everything.
Though the world outside is angry enough to burst,

this city's people are silent, exactly as silent

as the ruins on August sixth.

—AUGUST 1952

RHM: The National Police Reserve (1950–52) was one of two predecessors
of the Self-Defense Forces, established in 1954. The line about the silence of
the *hibakusha* may surprise the reader, but it was many years after the war
before the dropping of the bomb became a political issue, and many *hiba-
kusha* remained silent their entire lives (see "The Future Begins Here"
below).

Ground Zero

The city teems with a false prosperity.
This spot is our native place.
Scorched and broken as on that day,
the dome still stands exposed to wind and rain,
the rivers run full with memories of that day.
I come here, and strange to say,
my heart knows peace.

This spot is our place of birth.
This spot is our point of departure.
I come here
and hear the voices of the dead.

Hijiyama

Hijiyama, filled
with all our many dreams!
American ABCC atomic research station
towering there!
American scientists
beside the cool and gleaming instruments inside,
stripping us, taking pictures of our keloids,
compiling our case histories!
As you measure
with care
the scars of the atomic bomb
your country dropped
and record the number of white corpuscles it destroyed,
you feel no pain at all.

The sadness of our Hiroshima keloids,

ugly and twisted,

and our groans:

have you recorded even one person's share

and reported it home?

Hijiyama, filled

with all our many memories!

Though spring has come, the rows of cherry trees

that were burned out put forth leaves

but do not grow lush.

Hijiyama, turned to ruins

along with our youth!

The Stars and Stripes

flutters in the wind at your peak,

but baring your burned sides,

you send us a silent appeal.

Bridges

Like rainbows overhead, the bridges describe steel arcs

linking two shores

and dream of happy tomorrows.

One after another, the bridges bridge

the sevenfold river that swallowed tens of thousands

of people

and bring the surviving residents into contact.

The bridges hang above that day's river,

and people crossing them stop,

look down, call out.

The hair of the dead waves

about their broken faces, like duckweed,

their entrails sway to and fro, like ribbons,

and the dead speak even now
of the doomsday flash, flames, blood, screams.

From ancient times the bridges linked shore to shore
and brought people cut off from each other into contact.
Hiroshima is tomorrow's bridge of the heart
that connects people of different nations.

—August 1952

RHM: The opening lines contrast the city at large with Peace Park—"this
spot." Hijiyama is a prominent hill within Hiroshima's city limits and east
of Peace Park; it is the site of the ABCC, the Atomic Bomb Casualty Com-
mission (1947–75), which in 1975 became the Radiation Effects Research
Foundation.

THE GREEN OF HIROSHIMA

From scorched black skeletons of trees,
tender shoots reach out in all directions
and, weaving a brilliant green,
billow in the breeze.

The sun shines brighter,
roots deep in Hiroshima's sand
suck up the blood of that day,
leaves emit
what simmers inside the trees,
irradiating the city of the atomic bomb.

The ashes of death that blew in the wind
still pain them,
each time bombs explode over desert or ocean
their branches click with worry:
the green of Hiroshima that must not fade,
the trees of Hiroshima that must not die

add new rings each year
to the scorched rings
and become a vivid green flame
burning back at the sun.

—MAY 1960

THE HIROSHIMA NO ONE SERENADES

O Hiroshima
no one serenades—
turn a blind eye
to the charred scenes on the walls of the secret chamber,
    damp and dark,
and heave black sighs.
But the pain of that summer day
never fades.
Seek out the other Hiroshima,
fix it with a stare:
"Your eyes—
how can they be clear
as a summer lake?
I'd like
to gouge out your eyes
and get to the emptiness inside.
You and I—
we both were exposed to the flames.
I love you, I hate you."
O Hiroshima
no one serenades,
underneath the Hiroshima people do serenade.
Songs of Hiroshima born from its wounds
just as green trees stretch out branches
amid the rubble.
Serenades of Hiroshima
echo in the plaza,
the bloodsmeared faces of that summer day
never fade from the surface of the river. . . .

O sealed-off Hiroshima

no one serenades,

underneath the Hiroshima people do serenade—

refracting in my soul

and with that summer day

piercing my soul.

But

I sing—

for myself and for the other me.

—July 1960

RHM: The secret chamber with scenes on the wall of nuclear destruction is
a metaphor for the grim, enclosed world of the *hibakusha*. Kurihara sets that
Hiroshima against the Hiroshima of glittering modern buildings and has
the two converse. In the final stanza, the poet reenters the picture.

DIALOGUE

The atomic bomb museum here
in Peace Park, a birdcagelike structure
suspended above an arcade.
In the plaza
sandwiched between museum and cenotaph,
    green grass grows;
here flags wave,
placards bristle,
singing voices echo,
and doves fly
above great flushed crowds.
But this museum
is the land of the dead.
Suddenly I'm back
in the Hiroshima of August sixth:
a photograph
of an aid station, people lying about
painted with white salve,
bodies burned all over
and oozing fluid.
Male? female?—half-naked, naked,
turning to mush,
and groans resounding
inside a dark building.
Fossil-like among the rocks
fused with the rubble,
burned white bones.
Copper coins
fused into a lump.
Banknotes now ash.

Barbed wire melted into a tangle.

Cosmetics jar melted like jelly.

Liter bottle flattened.

Red-black lumps of keloid

preserved in alcohol.

Ah. These are the remains of the Hiroshima

that in one instant went up in flames.

With each year that passes,

the atrocity

grows blacker,

increases our anguish.

The museum here

in Peace Park

facing the cenotaph:

the dialogue between museum and cenotaph

never ends.

—AUGUST 1960

RHM: Peace Park includes the cenotaph, an eternal flame, a grassed-over mound marking the mass grave of thousands, the atomic bomb museum, a large fountain, a modern conference center, and many lesser monuments. The atomic dome is just to the east of Peace Park, across one arm of the Ōta River. The museum exhibit is on the only floor of the building, which stands on pillars that create an open arcade. See "Door to the Future."

PAINTING

A black lavalike substance flows
over the entire painting,
countless fallen forms
writhe in that mushy black lava,
and beneath the writhing forms
unmoving shapes lie in piles,
like heaps of rags.
In the monochrome smeared all over—
no time
or place,
no plants or flowers,
the only sound:
the groans of the trapped.

Everything has come to an end,
and there is silence: no one hoists the flag of truce,
no one digs graves.
Bases in far countries
have burned to ash,
beribboned generals
no longer put in appearances.

Those who yesterday
sat around happy tables
and exchanged gentle greetings—
"Daddy!"
"Mommy!"
"Kids!"—
now are a sea of naked bodies
painted a monochrome black.

No time

or place,

no plants or flowers,

just blood-colored flames blazing here and there.

—NOVEMBER 1962

RHM: The painting in question is the work of Maruki Iri and Maruki Toshi
(see John Dower and John Junkerman, eds., *The Hiroshima Murals: The Art of
Iri Maruki and Toshi Maruki* [Tokyo: Kodansha International, 1986]).

VOID

That? Oh, that.
Saddle-shaped void
standing in the full rays of the hot sun.
Enshrined within, a stone coffin.

People leveled the burned bones,
built a park,
planted memorial trees.
Adding sad rings each year, the trees
compose gorgeous green leaves,
and sparkling against the leaden sky,
the fountain transforms the dark curse
      into translucent drops of water.
But nothing can ever fill it,
the saddle-shaped void.
Since that day, there is a great void
in the hearts
of the people of this city, too,
that nothing can ever fill.

That? Oh, that.
Saddle-shaped void
standing there burning in the heat of the shimmering sand.
First altar,
dedicated to our fathers, mothers, children.
In front of it we vowed
that the mistake shall not be repeated,
but you—you didn't take the vow.
I see jetting missiles piercing

Japan's sky

and sunflowers turning to yellow dust and crumbling away.

That? Oh, that.

Saddle-shaped void,

lamp-lit and casting a shadow all night long.

People come here from all over the world

to fill the void in their hearts

and go home,

void still unfilled.

—FEBRUARY 1964

RHM: "Saddle-shaped" is an epithet often applied to the cenotaph. The image that arises more readily to an American consciousness is the canvas top of a Conestoga wagon, except that the cenotaph slants out, not in, as the sides approach the ground. The inscription reads, "Rest in peace. The mistake will not be repeated." Because of its vagueness, it has been the subject of much criticism, and some on the political right have sought to erase it entirely. See also "Nevada, 1" and "America: Don't Perish by Your Own Hand!"

RIVER

1. Mountains and River

Majestic mountains linked one to the next,
mountain ranges spreading out
sharp, tall, heavy, large,
villages cut off from the sun by jagged mountains,
in deep shade even during the day,
beneath the fluttering wings of birds,
indigo blue headwaters—
      headwaters—
stream murmuring in meadows at the foot of mountains
and flowing through maple forests—
      flowing—
breaking over rocks and throwing up spray—
      throwing up spray,
spray falling back into the flow
and flowing on to eternal tomorrows.

2. River of Memory

Mirroring sky, mirroring mountains,
full of human joys and sorrows,
flowing, flowing,
from the distant, distant past,
strumming gently
the dawns and dusks of riverside villages—
O river where in our youth
we angled for carp and dace
and scooped red minnows from the shallows.
River flowing so clear,
sweetfish, silver arrows,

swimming in schools.
Living in a harsh world,
we long for the river—the river.
O river our mother!
O river! O river our mother!
O river our mother, tell us:
what is the meaning of life?

3. Flood

Cooled in its waters, cherries blossom, trees flourish
in villages along the river,
and the river flows gently—
    gently through riverside villages—
flows abundantly.
When sweetfish come downstream
and rice tassels form,
the sky will cloud over without warning:
a storm blowing up out of the south.
In the blink of an eye
the river turns muddy, rises,
and, snarling like a tornado,
rushes madly past;
eroding mountains, dashing against rocks,
the river roars crazily,
cuts dikes,
flows through paddy and field,
destroys every trace—every trace—of plant and tree.
The setting sun shines down
on people lingering in ruined villages,
the rice does not ripen,
the festival drums do not sound,
the villages are silent.

Cool, clear, the river rolls on—
    rolls on.

4. Dried-Up River

What is life?
Something without end, always moving forward.
The river, too, is a living thing
that has flowed for eons.
It does not stop, but the ships
that used to ply it are no more;
the white sails filled with wind—
dream? reality?
The water at the base of the mountains dries up—dries up,
and in the riverbed below the mountains,
river shrinks to rivulet.
What is that sound in the parched, parched riverbed—
frog? insect?

5. War

War—
vain undertaking
when blood flows like a river,
the flowing blood is sucked down into the sand,
and friend and foe join in mutual hate.
That day, too, the river flowed clear,
and as summer day began,
the brilliant light flashed:
instant of silence in which day turned to night,
buildings blew away,
and amid swirling flames
mother and child called to each other;
sky, river,

city

all burned—all burned.

6. River's Rebirth

Rain falls on the ruined city,

wind blows in the ruined city,

and white bones—bones—lie about like seashells.

Autumn comes to the ruined city,

plants regain color,

freshness;

river mirrors blue sky,

heals wounds;

bridges: arcs of steel suspended

over sevenfold river—river.

Peace Bridge, round suns of its handrails

conversing with the sun.

Flowing water mirrors dome;

eternal echo—

the mistake will not be repeated.

"In the twenty years since that day,

he passed on, and so did she.

At dawn I heard the faint sound of insects."

"Nights by the great river

are beautiful.

I'm glad I'm alive."

I'm glad I'm alive,

I'm glad I'm alive:

those who sang that tune—

they, too, are now dead.

O sevenfold river

flowing gently, slowly, through the city of rivers,

O current

creating our future once again.
Carry our joys and sorrows,
flow without cease,
flow forever,
forever, forever
without end.

—NOVEMBER 1966

RHM: The Ōta River that flows through Hiroshima splits into the seven rivers that Kurihara compares (in "City under Ground") to "a keloid hand opened out." On Kurihara's authority I have translated *gigira* "red minnow." Peace Bridge was designed by noted architect Tange Kenzō; its handrails end in sculpted discs representing the sun.

OUR CITY

Engraved on our hearts,
the city we lost
is burned black as a negative,
and the river running through it
shines white as it flows to the sea,
reflecting the rays of the cruel August sun.

United in sympathy,
the injured
leveled bones and rubble
and built shacks of burned tin.
They sowed seed,
planted trees,
and resumed their human rounds.

Now Hiroshima
swallows the surrounding towns
and plans for the future megalopolis.
But what's there
is a dying landscape—
green belt wilted to brown,
sky and river both stagnant
from the huge waste and excretion
     of vast amounts of capital.
In that landscape people become small and light
     as grains of sand
and are tossed about;
even if they gnash their teeth and cry out,
their voices don't carry

but bump into the unfeeling walls of buildings
and die out.

Let's bring color back
to our city—
sun,
greenery,
river.
Let's set human songs singing.
Let's indict
those who would turn back history;
let's join with the dead underground
to hail with ringing voices
the world's dawn.

—AUGUST 1972

DOOR TO THE FUTURE

This is the door to the future.
This is the graveyard of humanity,
its concrete roof a flowing arch ten feet high.
In the foreground is the museum of the first tragedy,
and through the arcade beneath it
the fountain glitters whitely,
like a mercury lamp.
When no one is noticing, the dead—
burning with thirst even now—
slip out of the stone sarcophagus to drink
          the dripping water.

This is the door to the future.
People from all over the world
come here nonchalantly,
cameras dangling from their necks,
come here in fact to see with their own eyes
their own end.
Lovers stand pale and speechless
before the museum's bones
melted like jelly
and fused to metal and glass utensils;
mothers hold tighter
to their children
lest they too be burned to death.

This is the door to the future.
Can the world pass through this door
and bring back to life
these carbonized human ruins?

In a gloomy display room
a single stray dove
perches on the windowsill, its head tilted.

—JANUARY 1975

I SAW HIROSHIMA

"Hiroshima Mon Amour"

You saw nothing in Hiroshima.
Hiroshima: city of buildings and cars.
Couples in blue jeans snooze
on benches in the park,
a small child frolics with the pigeons on the grass.
The atomic dome,
the cenotaph—
they're only backdrops for snapshots.

No, this is what I saw.
People sitting in a group, like ascetics,
on the pavement in front of the cenotaph.
Moving not at all
and silent,
tuned into underground nuclear tests
in the deserts of far, far countries
and the soundless sound
of death ash blowing overhead,
people who once saw atomic hell.
People sitting on the pavement
and conversing with the dead,
joining with the dead
to call for peace.

This is what I saw.
People in Hiroshima
sitting on the pavement
and calling for peace.

—NOVEMBER 1977

PRAYER FOR A NUCLEAR-FREE TOMORROW

—For Kazuko

The forty-fourth August is here,
and the field of rubble
has become a city of gleaming buildings
ablaze in the summer sun.
The last structures from that time vanish
one by one,
and atomic bomb sites
become myths of Hiroshima man.

The drama of birth at the dawn of the atomic era,
in the hellish dark basement
of a shattered building,
has been engraved on the monument
to be unveiled August sixth.
To unveil the monument:
she who was born in that basement.
The mother who gave birth,
the midwife who helped with the birth,
the people who forgot their own pains to assist them—
they have all
departed this world.

But she who was born
at the very moment of the bomb
has become the mother of a dear child,

and with a prayer for a nuclear-free tomorrow,

she unveils a new age.

—JULY 1989

RHM: Kazuko is Kojima Kazuko. The building that Kurihara's poem "Let Us Be Midwives!" made famous was razed in 1988. On 6 August 1989 a monument was dedicated; the monument includes a photograph of the old building and the full text of "Let Us Be Midwives!"

JAPAN

THE FLAG, I

As if nothing at all had gone wrong,
the flag fluttered once more
high over the roofs
and began to dream again of carnage in broad daylight.
But no one looked up to it,
and people resented its insatiable greed
and gnashed their teeth at its monstrous amnesia.

Beneath that flag
each morning,
dizzy from malnutrition,
we were made to swear the oath of slaves
and, waving that flag, send off
fathers and brothers
wearing red sashes.
Ever since it flew over ramparts on the continent,
that flag has believed fanatically in the dream of empire.
From far Guadalcanal
to the cliffs of Corregidor.
It drove our fathers and husbands
into the caves of Iwojima and Saipan,
starved them like wild beasts,
and scattered their white bones.

Ah! Red-on-white flag of Japan!
The many nightmarish atrocities carried out at your feet.
Manila and Nanjing, where they splashed gasoline
over women and children
and burned them alive—
consummate crimes of the twentieth century.

Yet today the flag flutters again, shameless,
all those bloody memories
gone;
fluttering, fluttering in the breeze,
it dreams once more of redrawing the map.

—JUNE 1952

RHM: Shortly after the surrender, Japan's Ministry of Education prohibited the flying of the flag. General MacArthur eased the prohibition in 1947, allowed the flag to be flown on holidays in 1948, and abolished all restrictions in his New Year's message of 1950.

PEACE EDUCATION ARRESTED

—Incident at the Takamatsu Curriculum
Revision Council

I saw it.
Hundreds of police
filling the whole TV screen.
Waves of flat-topped Nazi hats.
Storming into the line of picketers,
the Nazi hats converge with the headbands;
both sides push, jostle,
throw, kick, scratch,
shove;
grabbed by hand or foot and pulled out,
three are handcuffed at the wrist.
O clear quiet eyes of the young teachers
who stand there linked and elated!

Not looking their young colleagues in the eye,
teachers enter the lecture hall.
You people:
since the war ended,
you have taught our children
respect for humankind,
avoidance of blind obedience,
truth and peace;
you pledged:
"We'll never send our students to war again."
Now the ethics of the teachers collapse with a roar.

According to those in charge,
"Not a single person was absent;
the session on the revision of the curriculum

opened one hour early

and ended without incident."

Really?

Really?

O clear quiet eyes of the young teachers

in handcuffs!

O peace education arrested!

The ethics of the teachers collapse with a roar.

The children you taught

are growing up bright and beautiful,

but teachers: please don't go back

to the road we once took.

—August 1958

RHM: During the Korean War the teachers' union pledged not to send Japanese pupils to war again.

RIVER OF FLAMES FLOWING THROUGH JAPAN

—Fifth World Convention, 1959

Scorching sun,
fifty-meter-wide highway, hot air and dust swirling up.
Young people burned by the sun
holding up their broad white banners—
oppose nuclear arms, outlaw nuclear bombs.

Red flags, green flags fluttering,
the peace march stretches on and on,
flowing like a river of flames.
The voice over the loudspeaker in the lead car:
"That day, too, was hot like today.
Hiroshima became one vast flaming plain.
Charred black
like burned cotton padding,
our brothers died."
.   .   .
Ambulances of the Japan Red Cross
follow along, slowly.
Women's groups waiting with cool barley tea.
City folk out in welcome,
filling both sides of the road.
Men, women, oldsters, youngsters—
all wave small green flags,
clap their hands,
wipe away tears that overflow.

Five-colored tape
is hurled from the windows of tall buildings,
and the tape they all reach for

connects them all.
Sweat and tears make things damp,
and tears overflow no matter how often
    people wipe them away.
". . . that day on this highway
we're now walking on,
on the side roads you're now standing on,
relatives who burned to death
lay fallen in heaps.
The fierce noonday sun
burned down on them. . . ."
The lead car's loudspeaker remembers.
". . . and even today, fourteen years later,
they're still dying
of atomic bomb disease
brought on by radiation. . . ."

People carry in front of them
photographs of brothers and friends who died.
The procession reaches Aioi Bridge, and—
There they are! There they are!—the grand procession
    of Tokyo and Niigata marchers
is crossing Honkawa Bridge.
Onward, onward,
flags, flags, flags—red and green;
rousing the people of towns and villages
of the eastern seaboard,
of the Japan Sea coast,
being welcomed by brothers,
joining hands,
holding rallies;
the grandmother who,
together with those who joined along the way,

climbed hand-in-hand with her grandson as far as the pass.
And the girl unable to join who offered
       her toy ring instead.
The procession stirred up
the quiet mountain folk
who had never once seen
the red flag pass by;
at the Japan Sea coast meeting to outlaw nuclear weapons,
it expressed fierce outrage
and passed a resolution of protest
against the Hiroshima Prefecture's Jimintō members
       who had trimmed their subsidy.
Fifty-six days on the road,
1,500 kilometers, like a river of flames
       flowing through Japan,
walking under the fiery sun,
walking in the rain and through storms,
walking stony roads,
countless blisters forming on the soles of feet,
the skin breaking and bleeding—
ah, today they've made it here:
Hiroshima's ground zero.
A great cheer wells up.
A storm of applause—
Welcome! Welcome, brothers!
And at that moment
the western delegation enters the site.
On June sixteenth
it left Okinawa's Yoron Island,
and with the Okinawan contingent at its head
walked 1,300 kilometers in fifty days,
the people's hopes swirling and flowing
like a river of flames.

Meandering loosely in from the three directions,
here before the cenotaph they converge.
Ah, focusing the hopes
of their hundred million Japanese brethren,
the Fifth World Convention Against Atomic and Hydrogen
        Bombs
gathers here at ground zero.

When they left Yoron Island, I hear,
their Okinawan brethren
set a signal fire at Hedomisaki across the water
and from Yoron Island, too,
a signal fire—
to pray for the success of the peace march.
Our imprisoned brothers: who can forget them?
—all of Okinawa an American base,
they have to cross barbed wire
and be checked and questioned
even just to work their fields.
Repeal the new death penalty!
Stop the revision of the Security Treaty!
As the attempt is made to turn atomic victim nation
        into victimizer nation,
the dead toss in their graves:
ceremony in front of the cenotaph at ground zero
on the night before the Fifth World Convention
        Against Atomic and Hydrogen Bombs.
Brass band blaring;
embracing on the platform:
two representatives—
American and Soviet.
In the crisscross of TV lights,
the world focuses for a moment on Hiroshima,

and the high point comes.

White doves are released—hundreds, thousands.

For a long while they circle low

over ground zero,

then finally disappear into the evening sky.

—AUGUST 1959

RHM: Jimintō is the Liberal Democratic Party, Japan's dominant political party, conservative in tendency. *The New York Times* covered this entire convention—with no mention of the march—in a single, one-inch entry on 4 August 1959. The report was fifty words long and ran on p. 24 (the final sports page), at the bottom of column 4 between a photograph of women's tennis and a report on a bridge tournament.

BENEATH THE SAME SKY

—The students and police of *Anpō*

It is not friend and foe
who inflict injury on each other;
it is not the blood of friend and foe
that is shed;
it is fellow countrymen
who drown in blood. . . .
You attack us
with helmets and nightsticks;
we hold you off
with placards.
What sets you and us
at each others' throats?

You
armed with helmets and pistols:
do you know
—that when the atomic bomb fell on Hiroshima,
thousands of soldiers
were charred black and died, helmets and all?
—that in the rubble of the parade ground, still as death,
exposed with the bones
for months
to sun and rain,
lay countless rusting red helmets?

What do you think will happen
after you with your helmets and nightsticks
spill our blood
and silence us?

For we and you
live beneath the same sky,
and neither we nor you
can escape
our shared fate.

—July 1960

RHM: *Anpō* is the security treaty joining the U.S. and Japan, signed in 1952 as the price Japan paid for the San Francisco Peace Treaty. On its revision and extension in 1960, popular opposition led to the greatest mass demonstrations of postwar Japan. The government succeeded in getting the treaty ratified, but the cost was high: President Eisenhower cancelled his scheduled visit—what would have been the first visit to Japan by an American president in office, and Prime Minister Kishi Nobusuke resigned soon after.

QUESTION

Burning, flames shooting
from eyes, mouth, nose,
hands joined in prayer: a monk.
Dyed the same flame-color,
the men and women encircling him
also join their hands in prayer.
The flames illuminate the black and tattered leaves
of trees scorched by napalm;
the entire paddy, too, is burned black.

We have been burned,
but we've never set ourselves afire in protest;
always passive,
we've been dragged slithering along
until now there are bases all over the Japanese archipelago,
and as the death stench of Vietnam envelops us,
nuclear submarines enter port,
and Japanese crows hungry for a target greet them.

Have you burned your draft card?
We have died
for the emperor,
but we haven't died to oppose war.
"Peace,
peace"—
launched lightly, like foam:
Japan's "peace."
Deep down inside:
the dead, settled heavily to the bottom,
the ghost city, burned like black sap.

—MARCH 1966

NO RESTING IN PEACE BENEATH THE FLAG

—In Peace Park

Do away with all pomp;
reject all delusion.
The green of the trees—it too burned that day,
not one leaf spared.

Over there—is it a dead horse, bloated?
An air-raid shelter made of sandbags?
A mock-up of the lonely huts
of burned tin roofing
erected in the atomic desert?
A *haniwa* mound dedicated to the dead
in the manner of our distant ancestors?
No: cenotaph with saddle roof, flowing
        and close to the ground.
When was it that the ceremonial pole was raised,
almost hidden among the trees just behind?
One day I saw the flag fluttering atop it.
Can the dead rest in peace
beneath a flag pregnant with unfulfilled ambition?
Through the museum arcade,
the navy march that resounds through the city
is audible even here.

Do away with all pomp;
reject all delusion.
This is the garden of the dead to which,
        over the five bridges,
come the people of the world.

This is the world's darkest abyss.

People stand at its edge

but can't see it.

—OCTOBER 1968

RHM: *Haniwa* mounds refer to the "keyhole" tombs of the prominent dead of the Tomb era (ca. A.D. 400). The flagpole was erected by a right-wing group on 29 April 1965.

WHEN WE SAY "HIROSHIMA"

When we say "Hiroshima,"
do people answer, gently,
"Ah, Hiroshima"?
Say "Hiroshima," and hear "Pearl Harbor."
Say "Hiroshima," and hear "Rape of Nanjing."
Say "Hiroshima," and hear of women and children in Manila
thrown into trenches, doused with gasoline,
and burned alive.
Say "Hiroshima,"
and hear echoes of blood and fire.

Say "Hiroshima,"
and we don't hear, gently,
"Ah, Hiroshima."
In chorus, Asia's dead and her voiceless masses
spit out the anger
of all those we made victims.
That we may say "Hiroshima,"
and hear in reply, gently,
"Ah, Hiroshima,"
we must in fact lay down
the arms we were supposed to lay down.
We must get rid of all foreign bases.
Until that day Hiroshima
will be a city of cruelty and bitter bad faith.
And we will be pariahs
burning with remnant radioactivity.

That we may say "Hiroshima"
and hear in reply, gently,

"Ah, Hiroshima,"
we first must
wash the blood
off our own hands.

—MAY 1972

INDICTMENT OF JAPAN

In Japan
there is a city where black rain falls, still invisible
(in that city nothing ever happens except that
abstract monuments and buildings
are forever going up),
but they say no one has seen the crooks.
The mayor likes ceremonies:
in summer, before the cenotaph,
he proclaims to the world
"a new order with no killing,"
and in the fall he stands on the reviewing stand
reviewing the troops
and encouraging killing.

In Japan
there are countless beaches and valleys
where resentment swirls black as tar.
Criminal factories go into operation
(though the crooks are in plain sight,
they cannot be arrested),
spew poison,
and fish and shellfish putrefy and dissolve.
People shuffle along in pain,
dance like cats,
and die frenzied deaths.
And at points all along the shoreline
are places that turn the sky blood-red night and day,
and people inhale the cloudy gas
cough horribly,
turn yellow, and die.

In the sea to the south of Japan
there is an island
where poison gas and nukes lie concealed under the briers
and even the sun is American-made.
The gangsters that twenty-eight years ago
starved the islanders,
gave them handgrenades,
and forced them into mass suicides
land once more,
wearing green camouflage suits,
and say they're there to defend the islanders.

The Japanese archipelago has grown overheated,
and the landscape is stained the color of blood;
still night and day
a stuck record
sings over and over,
"Everything's just fine!"
"Everything's just fine!"
In 1973 the summer of the defeat has grown distant,
and things have come full circle—
Japan now the seventh largest military power,
defense budget in the billions.
In the distance I hear the wolflike howls
of democrats who have grown fangs,
and I cannot rest.

Who are they,
who were they—the order-givers
who deserted brave underlings in the jungle
and have lived twenty-eight years snug and warm?
What was my own purpose in life during those years?

And what am I doing now?
We can't let the dead
be killed once again.

—JANUARY 1973

RHM: On the mayor who likes ceremonies, see also "Nippon: Piroshima."
Japan's pollution diseases include Minamata disease and itai-itai disease.
The island south of Japan is Okinawa, which in April and May of 1945 was
the scene of brutal fighting between Japanese and American troops and of
mass suicides forced on Okinawan civilians by the Japanese military.

The red of the red disk—the blood of the people;
the white of the white ground—the bones of the people.
With each war
they hoisted high the flag of bones and blood,
spilled foreign blood, even that of women and children,
and left foreign bones to bleach.

War comes to an end,
and it becomes a flag of peace,
raised high
in the Olympics,
at Asian jamborees;
each time they win an event,
they play the anthem,
and the criminal flag
that sucked the blood of millions,
that left the bones of millions to bleach,
flutters shamelessly.
"May the Imperial Reign last a thousand ages,
eight thousand ages. . . ."—
in that cause the people must shed their blood
and become bleached bones.
Even now the bones of those who never came back
lie bleaching in the fields and hills of Asia.

But has everyone
forgotten already?
—the bones of the 10,000 Chinese in the pit
—the bones that lie bleaching
on southern islands

—the hunger as we ate soybean cake,

locusts, and potato leaves

—the lice that bred

when children were sent off

to the country away from their mothers

—the families holding their breath

in air-raid shelters

on dark nights when the sirens sounded

—the 300,000 burned to death

in the atomic flashes.

Has everyone forgotten already?

Each night, after the last TV show,

they play the anthem,

and the flag of blood and bones

flutters and flutters.

The nation's entire day

is wrapped up in the flag.

It waves over City Hall

and over school playgrounds;

as if nothing at all had gone wrong,

it flutters

even over the cenotaph in Peace Park.

The red of the red disk—the blood of the people;

the white of the white ground—the bones of the people.

Even if the Japanese forget,

the peoples of Asia will never forget.

—SEPTEMBER 1975

RHM: "May the Imperial Reign . . ." is the opening of Japan's de facto national anthem; its origin is a poem the tenth-century *Kokinshū*.

THE FLAG, 3

Unhealed even now,
the tribe of the burned
lives its life in concentric cirles
about the saddle-shaped cenotaph.

The everyday life of their city of rivers
suddenly is assailed;
creating the uproar—
a swirling line of armored cars
flying the flag and the navy ensign,
dashing straight ahead,
making a U-turn, a tight full circle.
Volume turned up full blast,
they play the anthem and the battleship march,
set off firecrackers, roar in anger—the fascists.

Clad in similar navy-blue field gear, the riot squad
uses neither its water hoses
nor its tear gas.

People passing by
frown
and think of the dark forces
instigating these mercenaries.

Meeting in a gym blessed with soundproof walls,
the teachers swear an oath
to the people of the city of rivers:
"We'll never send our pupils to war again."

—JUNE 1976

This poem was given at the annual convention of the Japan Teachers'
Union.

YASUKUNI

This is the spot
to which the blood-stained myth led.
The sea of blood boils up in anger,
the mountain of bones crunches and crackles,
and screams of resentment resound in the dark.

From the Aleutians in the north
to Bougainville and Guadalcanal far in the south.
The bloody map of the Greater East Asian
        Co-Prosperity Sphere that included
the Chinese mainland, of course,
and Australia
and Southeast Asia.
Urged for the sake of the lord of all the earth,
"Don't come back alive!"
stirred up—
"Be brave, soldiers of Japan!"—
millions of men
became corpses on land, corpses at sea:
"Oh, to die by the side of my lord!"
Going back in time, piles of corpses,
the human bullets of the wars with China and Russia.
With the defeat, the bloodstained illusion
was blown away,
and the god had his bloody mask torn off;
but he quickly donned his symbolic mask
and kept his throne.
In order to pacify the angry souls
of soldiers mobilized for his vast nightmare,
he enshrines them, seals them in with sacred rope

and performs rites of pacification:

be at rest,

be at peace.

The chief priest—their former commander-in-chief.

He who dreams once again of a bloodstained map

wants to use the dead

to mobilize one hundred million.

This is the spot

to which the bloodstained myth led.

This is the spot that proves we must not

    be lulled asleep again,

we must not sleep.

—February 1981

RHM: Yasukuni, in Tokyo, is where the souls of Japan's military dead are enshrined. The "symbolic mask" the emperor donned refers to the emperor's declaration (1 January 1946) that he was not a god and to his role as "symbol of state" in the postwar constitution. See also "Spring Has Come to Europe." "Oh, to die by the side of my lord!" is from the wartime song "Umi yukaba" (see note to "War Close Up," above).

FEBRUARY ELEVENTH, 1984

Orwell's 1984,
Nippon's 1984.
Pandora's box is open,
and once more you hear:
    "Tennō heika banzai!"
    "Tennō heika banzai!"
"Hirohitler *banzai!*"
"Hirohitler *banzai!*"
"Sixty years on the throne: *banzai!*"
"Tennō and 'My' Shōwa: *banzai!*"
Exalted national character, beyond compare;
one people, one language;
hegemon of the "eight corners of the world under one roof,"
hegemon of the world.
    "Heil Hitler!"
    "Heil Hitler!"
February eleventh, 1984:
flood the city with the flag and the anthem. . . .
Tramp! Tramp! Tramp!
Hut-two-three-four!
The celebration in Peace Hall in Peace Park
to which even Hiroshima's mayor sends a message.
Out of Pandora's box they all come flying:
presidents of the PTA, the medical association,
    corporations,
heads of Seichō no Ie, the Housewives' League,
    the Shrine Association,
the All Men Are Brothers Boat Racing League,
the League of Hiroshima Patriots, the Boy Scouts,
the Disabled Vets, the advocates of nuclear civil defense,

the former chief of the Defense Agency, defeated
    at the polls,
members of the prefectural assembly, city councillors,
    the head of the Chamber of Commerce,
Diet members—Liberal Democrat, Democratic Socialist,
    Clean Government.
Hut-two-three-four!
Onward! Onward!—
the sounds touch off dark forebodings.
Above the atomic cenotaph in Peace Park
the flag waves and flutters:
Die! Die for the Emperor!

—FEBRUARY 1984

RHM: The eleventh of February is Japan's Fourth of July (*kenkoku ki-nenbi*),the traditional date for the mythological founding of Japan. It was used in prewar indoctrination (under the name *kigensetsu*) and reintroduced in 1966. *Tennō heika banzai* is *banzai* for the emperor; "Hirohitler" is an expletive that protesters in Britain, West Germany, and the Netherlands used to greet Hirohito on his trip to Europe in 1971. "Eight corners of the world under one roof" is a phrase from prewar propaganda. Seichō no Ie [House of Growth] is one of Japan's "new" religions. Founded in 1930, it has roots in Shinto conservatism and was noted in the prewar and war years for its nationalism. Clean Government Party is the Kōmeitō, the political wing of Sōka Gakkai.

SPRING HAS COME TO EUROPE . . .

—Second poem to a friend in Nagasaki

The blood that fell on the pavement
when pistol shots rang out
is the red rose of liberty and democracy.

God gave him
life and breath and a mission.
Democracy had been napping, fat and happy,
but woke up at the sound of the pistol
and in cities and towns all over Japan began to stir.

Defeated in war, the emperor
disavowed the myth and declared himself human,
but should the day come when man turns god once again
and ascends the throne,
liberty and democracy
will not be asleep then.
Spring has come to Europe,
but Japan faces winter
once again.
Still, the globe
rushes toward spring.

—February 1990

RHM: On 24 January 1990 Motoshima Hitoshi, mayor of Nagasaki, was the
object of an assassination attempt, presumably by a right winger offended
by his statement that the Shōwa emperor bore responsibility for the Pacific
War.

WHAT DID THEY FIGHT FOR?

What did they fight for?
Whom did they fight for?
Neither husbands nor sons came back.
Nor did students.
In Hiroshima 200,000 were burned alive;
in Kure, 1,831 people were killed by bombs.

What did they kill for?
For whose sake were they killed?
Countless nightmares unfolded
beneath the red-on-white flag.
Asians slaughtered: twenty million.
Japanese dead at home and abroad: three million.

We pledged
that the mistake would not be repeated.
Article 9 renounces war.
But the minesweepers
flew the navy ensign
as they left port, seen off by waves of Hinomarus.

The first time may have been a mistake;
the second time will be perfidy.
Military city Hiroshima: don't bring it back!
Military harbor Kure: don't bring it back!
Don't turn guns on Asia once again!

—OCTOBER 1991

RHM: Japan contributed minesweepers (and $9 billion of the American cost
of $60 billion) for the Gulf War.

WORDS ARE WHERE IT STARTS

Long ago: *tennō*.
Today: *kōken*.
The media parrot what the government says,
and the words blanket the land.

When words inflate,
people who don't wish to think about their meaning
swallow them as is.
If asked on the street to sign a petition,
they sign, "Because it's *kōken*."
For the sake of *"kōken,"* sons and pupils
are sent off armed
to lands we once invaded.

People! Enough of such words!
When fraud, sophistry, and deceit
once again would pass for truth,
let's be like the noonday sun,
exposing the words of darkness
and showing what's what.

Words are where it starts.
Once it was *tennō heika banzai*.
Now it is *kōken banzai*.
Let's understand the key words.
"Global partnership,"
"burden-sharing,"
New World Order, New Greater East Asian
        Co-Prosperity Sphere,
Cambodia occupied by the United Nations:

it's not simply a matter of goods and money
but of shedding the blood of young Japanese.

You for whom words are all—
don't accept false words
and repeat the mistake.
Even if the first time was a mistake,
the second time is betrayal.
Don't forget our pledge to the dead.

—MAY 1992

RHM: "Long ago" is prewar, and *tennō* is emperor. *Kōken* is contribution, that is, the contribution of troops to U.N. peace-keeping missions, the focus of debate over a government proposal, passed in June 1992, to permit the sending of Self-Defense Forces abroad under the auspices of the United Nations. In stanza 2 Kurihara writes *kōken* first in characters, presumably because it is adults who are being asked to sign petitions in support of the draft legislation, then in syllables, presumably to indicate schoolchildren's lesser knowledge of characters. She writes "global partnership" and "burden-sharing" in phonetic equivalents of the English and provides Japanese translations in parentheses.

CHANGE

Land where the soul of language flourishes!
While poets were absorbed in flashy wordplay,
beasts took words
and changed everything.

"The world has changed,
so Japan too must change!"
"Time for CHANGE!" "Time for CHANGE!"
Shouting at the top of their lungs,
this party, that party,
all rush to jump on the bandwagon
of the New World Order Assistance Association.

We were first.
No, we were.
"No—*we* were first."
Resort to arms for peace—perfectly sensible.
Those who don't change—
out of date, old-fashioned.
"Time for CHANGE!" "Time for CHANGE!"
"Time for reform!" "Time for reform!"

A half-century ago
we sent fathers, sons, husbands, brothers off to war,
towns and villages all over Japan
were incinerated in the air raids,
and two cities vanished from the face of the earth.
Three million Japanese died;
twenty million Asians were slaughtered.
We pledged not to resort to arms again. And yet:

"Time for CHANGE!" "Time for CHANGE!"

Fifty years—high time for major reform!

They won't change what needs changing,

but they'd change

what should never be changed.

Land where the soul of languages flourishes!

While poets were absorbed in flashy wordplay,

beasts took words

and in the twinkling of an eye

changed everything.

RHM: Kurihara writes the noun "CHANGE" in English in capital letters seven times (including the title); she uses the Japanese verb "to change" nine times and the Japanese noun "reform" three times. The line "land where the soul of language flourishes" is from the *Man'yōshū*, although Kurihara writes *kotoba* (word) rather than *kotodama* (soul of language); *kotoba* appears four other times. The parties to which Kurihara refers are the Socialist and other opposition parties that gave up their resistance to the use of Japan's Self-Defense Forces on U.N. peace-keeping operations. The term "Assistance Association" is an allusion to the Imperial Assistance Rule Association, which during World War II amalgamated all existing political parties and rendered them powerless. It is Article 9 of the constitution that Kurihara thinks should never be changed.

EMPERORS, PRIME MINISTERS, MAYORS

HUMAN EMPEROR, MEEK AND MILD

He beams at puppies
and smiles sweetly—"Take care!"—
at old folks in rest homes
and war orphans,
he of the round shoulders, he whom the retarded children
    at Roppō School
call Grandpa:
human emperor, meek and mild.

But the Court sent maroon limousines especially
from Tokyo to Hiroshima,
day laborers and volunteers cleaned up
all the city streets,
and the prefecture appropriated millions of yen
for police with pistols and nightsticks,
killed four cows for his three-day stay—
gift-wrapping and refrigerating only what he himself
    would eat,
and awaited his arrival.

Disabled vets in dirty white,
arms and legs missing, call out in the streets,
and daughters of defeat
walk arm in arm with American soldiers.
Shacks of scorched sheet metal
and the dark swarm who live hand to mouth
have been cleared out by force,
and Hiroshima is a city
of high-rise buildings.

The emperor praises the city for having come back
beyond recognition,
but the only ones who've come back are
    the bloodsucking merchants of death.
Blown like leaves into piles,
living in shacks
huddled on riverbanks,
cupboards bare,
subsisting from day to day:
the clan of thin-blooded Hiroshimans.

Rumors are rampant of khaki-clad armies
crossing the straits to Korea,
and soon they'll try to turn our husbands and sons
into human bullets once more—
does he know?
Does he not know?
Round-shouldered,
he beams at puppies:
human emperor, meek and mild.

           —DECEMBER 1951

RHM: Here Kurihara uses the term *tennō* to refer specifically to the Japanese
emperor. This poem is Kurihara's earliest use of strong sarcasm. "Human
bullets" (*nikudan*) is an expression for do-or-die soldiers that dates back to
Japan's wars at the turn of the century.

NIPPON: PIROSHIMA

I

The mayor of Piroshima
is an old fox
who likes to dress up in tuxedos.
Pulling on white gloves,
he gives speeches larded with English,
"*Piisu*." "*Piisu*."

The mayor of Piroshima
constructs a zoo
in Piroshima's back parlor,
invites rare beasts from all over the world,
and opens it to the public on August sixth.

August sixth, see,
is the day 200,000 people of Hiroshima
were broiled to death by rays,
the day the seven rivers filled with corpses,
the day a great swarm of people fled,
torn flesh hanging,
and died in agony by the road.

For the mayor of Piroshima,
August sixth is a grand memorial service for blowfish.
This—the day that commemorates the corpses with torn flesh
     piled up,
soaked with gasoline, cremated.
May their souls find rest. "*Piisu*." "*Piisu*."

His address goes out via radio
to the whole world.
A grand, grand ceremony.

To please the children,
he trots out a two-humped camel and a black rhino,
and to scare the adults
he summons
from Tokyo
a bug-eyed monster
to give a speech from the dais.
Nippon: Piroshima—
Ha. Ha. Ha.

2

The mayor of Piroshima
is an old fox
who likes to dress up in tuxedos.
Pulling on white gloves,
he gives speeches larded with English,
"Piisu." "Piisu."

Several years ago
the mayor of Piroshima wanted to rebuild
Piroshima's old Supreme Command,
so that it and the atomic dome could coexist.
On the great *torii* of the shrine
        where the Supreme Command once stood
you can see even now the name of its donor,
        Lieutenant General so-and-so.

In the summer,
the mayor of Piroshima stands before
    the saddle-shaped cenotaph,
has the bells rung and the doves released,
and reads his address.
"The mistake will not be repeated."
"*Piisu*." "*Piisu*."
In the fall
he reviews the line of heavy tanks and artillery
that rushes ahead toward the fourth five-year plan
and tramples on the layers of human bones
    beneath the cenotaph.
At that time the mayor of Piroshima
becomes the mayor of Fortress Hiroshima
and strikes a pose.

The mayor of Piroshima
is an old priest
in love with ceremonies.
The ceremony marking the twenty-sixth anniversary of the
    bomb,
the twenty-first annual review of the troops—
the same
high ceremony.
"The Self-Defense Force is not an army."
"Ours is a peace constitution,
so this is not militarism."
"Small-scale nuclear weapons
are not unconstitutional."
Nippon: Piroshima.
Nippon: Piroshima.

The old priest in love with ceremonies

will ceremony Hiroshima

to death.

—OCTOBER 1971

Part 1 of the poem was written in August 1971; part 2 in October 1971. The summer of 1971 marked Prime Minister Sato's first ceremonial visit to the atomic cenotaph.

RHM: The title of this poem in Japanese is *Nippon: Piroshima*, written phonetically in *katakana* rather than characters. *Nippon*, the harsher pronunciation of *Nihon*, "Japan," carries connotations of the war and militarism. *Piroshima* looks exactly like Hiroshima except that a small circle above the *Hi* turns it into the aspirated *Pi*. In the poem Kurihara moves from the aspirated *pon* of *Nippon*, to the *Pi* of *Piroshima*, to the *pi* of *piisu*, a phonetic representation of the English "peace," line 6. The strange beasts in stanza 2 presumably are VIPs from abroad. Blowfish are a culinary delight, the taste reinforced by the danger involved—improperly prepared blowfish livers are fatal. A service for blowfish would thank them for their usefulness to humankind, beg their forgiveness for humankind's use of them, and ask their forbearance in the future. The reference to blowfish resonates in at least two ways: its utter inconsequence compared with 6 August and a parallel with 6 August—the agony that blowfish poisoning causes its victims and the agony of atomic bomb deaths. Sato Eisaku, prime minister from 1964 to 1972, was a former Class A war crimes suspect. He was also a caricaturist's delight: heavy eyebrows and large eyes. Hiroshima's Supreme Command, a structure set up on the grounds of Hiroshima Castle and made use of only in time of war, served its intended purpose during the Russo-Japanese War; it was destroyed on 6 August.

THE NAKED EMPEROR

The emperor's weavers said,
"This is beautiful cloth;
only honest people can see it,"
and presented him cloth that wasn't cloth.
Thinking he was wearing beautiful clothes,
the emperor walked the city streets naked.
The people of the city all joined
in praising the clothes that weren't clothes:
"Pretty as a rainbow!"
But an honest child said,
"The emperor's naked!"

Now no matter how often
the emperor's weavers say,
"This cloth is the world's best,"
children and adults, too, all say,
"The emperor's naked!"
Only the emperor and his clan keep saying,
"The emperor is not naked," and
"He's wearing beautiful clothes."

Generals and scholars of the nation
that turned two cities to atomic desert
and burned to death 300,000 of their residents
attest that their warships
enter our harbors carrying nuclear weapons
and that nuclear weapons
are stored on the bases.
Still, the emperor says,
"They're not bringing in nuclear weapons."

And he neither checks the facts

nor protests.

Angry at the emperor and his clan who say

what isn't is

and what is isn't,

people throughout the land gather daily

for demonstrations and meetings

to protest against nuclear weapons.

"No more Hiroshimas!"

"No more Nagasakis!"—

the people of the two cities

whose parents, children, brothers and sisters

     were burned to death

live bursting

with anger and pain.

In towns and villages all over Japan,

the wind whispers,

"It's a lie, a lie, a lie!"

—OCTOBER 1981

RHM: This poem makes use of the Hans Christian Andersen tale, but in Japanese the "emperor" becomes a generic prince or ruler, not *tennō* but *ōsama*. For the wind, see the note to "His Majesty Has Donkey's Ears."

HIS MAJESTY HAS DONKEY'S EARS

Because no one said,
"His Majesty has donkey's ears,"
because those who said it were put in jail,
naive middle-schoolers and even young Koreans
whose country the emperor had taken by force
volunteered, were honored
as aces of sky and sea,
and left their bones to bleach in the seas and jungles
        of the far south
and on the plains of the continent.

No one said,
"His Majesty has donkey's ears,"
so, thinking His Majesty a god,
they called countries that disobeyed
        the divine country savage,
burned them out,
pillaged them,
murdered them,
and were awarded Orders of the Golden Kite.

No one could say,
"His Majesty has donkey's ears,"
so in order to save the throne, His Majesty
        did not surrender,
and bombs were dropped

on Hiroshima and Nagasaki,
and 300,000 residents were burned alive.

They lost the war,
and it finally became possible to say,
"His Majesty has donkey's ears."
His Majesty himself declared,
"I have donkey's ears."
Yet some uneducated people
were still under the spell—
"His Majesty is a god"—
and crafty politicians
began to chorus at the top of their lungs,
"His Majesty doesn't have donkey's ears"
and "His Majesty is a god."
So to turn sham soldiers
into His Majesty's soldiers,
they enshrined the shades
of sham soldiers who died in traffic accidents.
Widows who revered the spirits of dead husbands
and friends
joined forces to plead,
"His Majesty has donkey's ears,"
"I want my husband back," "I want my friend back."

His Majesty has donkey's ears.
Don't fall for the plot
to steal the people's lives and their history

and rewrite them as His Majesty's lives,

His Majesty's history.

His Majesty has donkey's ears;

he can't hear human words.

—FEBRUARY 1980

RHM: This poem makes use of the Greek myth about Midas. Judging a musical contest between Apollo and Pan, Midas inexplicably chose Pan. In punishment, an angry Apollo turned Midas' ears into the ears of an ass. To hide his new ears, Midas wore a turban, but he could not keep the secret from his barber. Knowing the danger of speaking, yet unable to keep silent, the barber dug a hole, whispered the secret into the hole, and filled the hole again with dirt. Whispering reeds grew up on that spot and, when the wind blew, betrayed the secret. Kurihara again uses *ōsama*, the generic term for king, but she is referring to the emperor. "Sham soldiers" is a contemptuous reference to the Self-Defense Forces that are without constitutional legitimacy. The Order of the Golden Kite is one of imperial Japan's military decorations. See Norma Field, *In the Realm of A Dying Emperor* (New York: Pantheon, 1991), 107–74, for an account of one widow who tried to prevent the enshrinement of her dead husband.

Chubby,

glossy face shiny with sweat,

the emperor of the new clothes,

his (nuclear) belly button plain to see,

says he's coming to Hiroshima.

He says he'll pay his respects at the atomic cenotaph.

Can he really stand

belly-button-bare before the monument

that says "the mistake shall not be repeated"?

The emperor of the new clothes,

who says what is isn't

and what isn't is

and turns lies and fraud into state policy,

says he's coming,

bare belly button and all.

In Hiroshima

not only the children

but also the old people, the men, the women

laugh, get angry

at the chubby emperor's

belly-button antics.

In April he pays his respects at the shrine to war,

in August he pays his respects at the atomic cenotaph.

Repeating flat contradictions every day,

in the country across the sea

he says what they want him to say;

here at home, for domestic consumption,

he says what is isn't

and what isn't is.

But Hiroshima will not be fooled.

O, you 200,000 dead!

Come forth, all together,

from the grave, from underground.

Faces swollen with burns,

black and festering,

lips torn,

say faintly, "We stand here in reproach."

Shuffle slowly forward,

both arms shoulder high,

trailing peeled-off skin.

Tell them—

the emperor of the new clothes

and his entire party—

what day August sixth is.

—AUGUST 1981

RHM: The chubby "emperor" is Suzuki Zenko, prime minister in 1981. The lines "what is isn't / and what isn't is" are a reference to the presence of nuclear weapons on American bases on Japanese soil. The "shrine to war" is Yasukuni Shrine; see "Yasukuni."

GOLD AND NUKES

Once upon a time
there was a king who loved gold.
He was given the power
to turn absolutely everything
he touched
to gold.
One day the king's young daughter
came to his room, cried, "Daddy,"
and threw her arms around him.
In his embrace
she turned to solid gold.

Nowadays
there are kings
who love nukes more than gold,
and they have been given the power
to destroy humankind
at the touch
of a button.
As if competing at soccer,
these kings
competed at testing
atomic bombs.
All over their countries
they wove fine nets of nuclear-bomb factories
and nuclear power plants.
The death ash
crossed borders and oceans
and spread throughout the world.

Gradually and surely, the bodies of those who absorb
            radiation
are eaten away
and develop leukemia and cancer,
their hair falls out, red spots appear,
they vomit blood and die.
Even so, the kings keep repeating that all is well:
"We can't be sure the one causes the other."

Just as the daughter of the king who loved gold
turned into a statue of gold,
the kings' daughters develop leukemia.
Even so, I doubt that the kings
will stop their game of nukes.
Babies in their cradles
all over the world
and children running about with bright smiles
will be burned black as charcoal,
and the globe will turn into a planet void of life
that can never again support life.
In the dark wind
uranium and helium
go on singing
their song without words.

—FEBRUARY 1982

THE DAY THE SHŌWA ERA ENDS

Deep inside the moat on which swans drift, oblivious,
the emperor is in pain,
now vomiting blood, now passing blood,
only dimly conscious.
Does he think of them?

Victims of the atomic bomb
lying on straw in sheds and stables
of the farms to which they fled
that summer's day forty-three years ago,
ridden with fever, trembling from chills,
breaking out all over in red spots,
hair falling out, no medical treatment of any kind,
not knowing even the name of their affliction,
who died with blood pouring from ears, mouths, noses;
victims of the atomic bomb who passed
     so much blood their bowels seemed to have melted,
who hadn't even rags to use as diapers,
who died drowning in blood.

Rallying with transfusion after transfusion,
hardly conscious,
does he mount his white horse
and wander distant battlefields?
The hell of starvation in island jungles
     of countries to the south,
on the cliffs of the continent,
that made people eat snakes, frogs, human flesh.
Soldiers wracked by malarial fevers,
shivering from chills

beneath the sizzling southern sun,

arms and legs blown away by naval artillery,

unable even to move,

who died on foreign soil—

as his life ebbs,

does he make a tour of inspection?

A single life should count more than the world;

one life should count for no more

than any other.

Yet counting for less than a feather,

those husbands and sons went to their deaths singing,

"At sea be my corpse water-soaked;

     on land let grass grow over it.

Let me die beside my lord."

Their one-time lord—while wandering the borderland

     between life and death,

does he make his way

to the battlefields of Greater East Asia

to hand out imperial gift cigarettes

and award Orders of the Golden Kite?

Even after the war ended

the one-time commander-in-chief

never showed contrition for his sins.

Will the Greater East Asian war finally come to an end

on the day the Shōwa era ends?

Or does Japan stand already

on the threshold of new war?

The voices of the cicadas that cried bitterly all over Japan in August forty-three years ago

resound now,

deafeningly loud.

—December 1988

RHM: This poem was Kurihara's contribution to an anthology of the same title, a collection of hostile poems composed during the Shōwa emperor's final illness. The quotation comes from *Kokinshū*.

THE WORLD

THE CROW

In the plaza with the arch-shaped gravestone
birds swarmed and chirped.
The birds had all turned white—
birds of prey with bills clipped,
long-tailed birds with tails clipped—
and chirped, "Unity," "Unity."
Under the sand they pecked at:
the silence of desolate layers of white bones.

We clustered chirping in the plaza:
"You—what sort of bird are you?"
"I—what sort of bird am I?"
My throat so dry it was on fire,
I thought I might lose my voice.
Call me a black crow if you like,
but crows want to sing crow songs.
"You were better off with your long tails!"
"You were better off flitting from branch to branch
singing your light songs!"

I am a black crow.
Singing my song,
I take flight for the far north.
There, a gravestonelike cloud gleams
the color of seashells.

—AUGUST 1961

RHM: In 1961 Kurihara denounced the Soviet Union's nuclear tests, but her
colleagues refused to do so. The "far north" refers to the Soviet Union.

NEVADA, I

—The resumption of nuclear testing by the U.S. and
the U.S.S.R.

Nevada!
Are you lighting once again
the fire of doom?
The Hiroshima
you hit the first time:
even today, suddenly, hair falls out,
gums bleed,
people vomit basins of blood,
pink spots come out like stars, and they die.

Nevada!
What should we do
about the seething anger
that wells up like bloody pus
under keloids scabbed over?
We are the ones who vowed,
"The mistake will not be repeated."
The one who needed to take the vow,
Nevada,
is you.

Nevada!
Can't you hear the sobs,
can't you hear the groans
from the ruined Hiroshima
that is your handiwork?
You who hold in your hands
a hundred thousand Hiroshimas,

don't your hands terrify you?
When a hundred thousand Hiroshimas
go up in flames at the same moment,
that will be the end
both for you and for the world. . . .

—OCTOBER 1961

SEMIPALATINSK, 2

Semipalatinsk,
Central Asia: the name
engraved for the first time onto my heart.
Like Nevada and Bikini,
a graveyard so sterile it will never come back to life.

No matter how beautiful the words
you use to speak of the future, at that moment
the sun stopped shining,
flowers withered,
neither birds nor butterflies took wing;
only the sinister mushroom cloud
floated in the air,
signature affixed to your act.
To orbit the earth seventeen times
in twenty-five hours and eighteen minutes—
vain orbiting.
From that orbit, you say,
you can set off jets of flaming hatred
and hit any place on earth.
By speaking of hundred-megaton hydrogen bombs,
haven't you hurled a hundred megatons of malice
at humankind?

Semipalatinsk,
Central Asia:
spitting fire, the serpent
touches off the energy of doom,
calls forth new explosions,
and beckons the end of the world.

—OCTOBER 1961

WHOM DID THEY FIGHT FOR?

Whom did they fight for?
What did they fight for?
The soldiers who went to battle
across the far far sea
went back across that sea,
home to their mothers.
They went home with bodies torn,
hollowed out.
The soldiers who shed their young blood
for an empty freedom
will probably drown those who sent them
in that sea of blood.
In the groves of Arlington
new graves increase by the day,
and American mothers take to the streets to call out,
"Don't send our sons to war!"
We who were burned by the atomic bomb
call out:
"Don't repeat Hiroshima
in Vietnam!"

DON'T GO TO THE U.S.A.!

Young people:
don't go to the U.S.A.!
Computers whir morning and night,
computers decide everything—
wars, presidents,
marriages, births.
But you can't comprehend Vietnam
with computers.
You can't pacify Black people with computers.
The hippies with their flowers are on the move.

Young people:
don't go to the U.S.A.!
They make you extend your visa every six months,
and each time you have to pledge
to become an American soldier.
Suddenly one day your call-up notice drops
        into your mailbox—
will you be able to climb into a helicopter,
land in a Vietnamese village,
throw a hand grenade
at a hut built of palm leaves,
burn women and children?

U.S.A., land of computers;
land where humans are dehumanized;
in return for six months washing dishes,
they notify you you're 1-A.

Land where vultures swoop down
and carry you off into distant wilds.

—OCTOBER 1968

RHM: The case of Shimizu Tetsuo provided the stimulus for this poem. A
hibakusha in Hiroshima as a baby, Shimizu traveled to the U.S. and was
drafted. Sent to Vietnam, he went AWOL in Japan and gained the support
of Kurihara and others. Under the military draft system then in force, 1-A
was the designation for the most eligible men—physically fit and with no
psychological or other impediment.

AMERICAN PIGWEED

Seen from a distance,
they are solid yellow
and call to mind fields of rapeseed—
the fallow fields of the new towns
adjoining the city caught up in a building boom.
Along the railroad tracks,
on banks of streams sluggish with industrial waste,
and also under the thatched eaves of silent farmhouses
left vacant when people went elsewhere
      for off-season work:
verdant, opening its yellow blossoms—
gangly lathergrass.

America—white moth
that eats up all the tender buds
and threatens to blight woods and forests;
gangly lathergrass
that sends down roots like underground stems,
discharges poison,
kills the indigenous plants,
and transforms even the landscape.

American pigweed:
it sets its frothy seeds to float all over Japan,
aggravates allergies,
and no matter how often you dig it up,
it sends out new life from roots you missed.

American pigweed:

a parasite throughout Japan—

Okinawa, Iwakuni, Misawa, Yokota—

ruining Japan.

—OCTOBER 1972

RHM: I have translated ragweed as "pigweed" and goldenrod as "lath-ergrass," the literal renditions of the terms in Japanese. Okinawa, Iwakuni, Misawa, and Yokota are major U.S. bases in Japan.

Thirty years ago this summer,
having destroyed the fascism
of Hitler and Mussolini
and occupied the emperor's Japan,
America glittered in triumph.
Now, its vaunted computers
of no use in Japan,
it licks the very dregs,
furls the tattered Stars and Stripes, and leaves.

It burned the plains of Vietnam,
burned the jungles,
burned the birds,
honeycombed human bodies
with cluster bombs,
and at the end used suffocation bombs
that left heaps of corpses of women and children
dead of suffocation, mouths agape like fish,
having shed no drop of blood.

The world's press
reviewed the war that ended:
meaningless deaths,
meaningless waste,
meaningless duration,
but not a single one
of the dead returns.
Worse, like beasts already avid for blood,
the newspapers lick their chops
at the thought that Korea is next.

In the south of the peninsula
the authorities prepare for new war
by executing one after another
those who resist,
and rivers of blood flow.
The American Secretary of Defense
threatens to use nukes
to defend the regime of torture and blood.
The atomic bomb thirty years earlier—
whom can it have defended against whom?
The army that was supposed to be dissolved
and the war criminals who were supposed to be purged
are all just the way they were.

Microcephalic children, now thirty years old,
want to marry,
turning their mothers' hair white.
Mothers wait even now
for children who set out that morning
and of whom not even a bone has turned up.
Hiroshima's war is still not over,
but the smell of gunpowder
envelops us anew.

—AUGUST 1975

AMERICA: DON'T PERISH BY YOUR OWN HAND!

—Protesting the atomic bomb air show

A generation has gone by,
the words on the stone coffin in Peace Park
have become a riddle from the distant past,
and people ask, "What mistake?"
and "Who won't repeat it?"
At an air show across the sea
they reenacted Hiroshima
and sent a mushroom cloud leaping
into the fall Texas sky.
Those who watched
were not burned in the flash,
were not covered with death ash,
were not soaked with tarlike
black rain.

Ah, the dead sucked up in the firestorm
and vaporized in the sky.
The dead pursued by the flames
who died in heaps on the riverbanks.
The dead cut off by curtains of fire
who burned alive.
The great mass of the dead whose corpses
were scorched in the hot August sun,
gave off a stench, and eddied blackly
above the burnt earth.
The dead whose bodies were heaved onto piles
like rubbish,
doused with gasoline, and burned.

The dead who dragged themselves on, strings of skin
      hanging off,
and drew their last breaths
while fleeing.
The dead girls who escaped safely
only to have their hair suddenly fall out, pink spots
appear like stars all over their bodies,
who died before dawn, vomiting blood.
One bomb brought all this about.
The Hiroshima in which day became night,
hot summer became cold summer,
the Hiroshima that became the end of the world—
its voice carried nowhere.

Even now the echoes of the atomic bomb do not fade.
In obscure corners of the building-boom city,
patients suffering radiation sickness
and *hibakusha* desperate to hide their keloids
live forgotten lives,
second and third generation suddenly die of leukemia,
and thirty-year-old microcephalics babble baby-talk,
bringing grief to aged parents.

We vowed
that the mistake would not be repeated.
It is the United States that must take the vow.
O America, you with the atomic bombs
to burn out Hiroshima a million times over:
don't perish by your own hand!
When a million Hiroshimas explode
in the U.S.A.,
Americans
won't have time to think, "Ah, Hiroshima,"

before they vanish into the air.

When that happens,

on behalf of the three hundred thousand dead

of Hiroshima and Nagasaki,

I will send a message of condolence to the United States.

You American heroes who say,

"I'll go wherever

the president orders me":

God may forgive

your mushroom-cloud hell,

but humankind will not.

—OCTOBER 1976

RHM: For an account of the Texas air show, see *Newsweek*, 25 October 1976, p. 59.

AMERICA: WORLD'S BEST IN EVERYTHING

—For Bikini

The United States prides itself on being #1,
world's best in everything.
In Hiroshima it designated
Kikkawa Kiyoshi—
keloids erupting like lava all over his back,
the five fingers of his right hand
fused together, twisted in,
cramped and unmoving—
atomic bomb victim #1.

On Rongelap,
on the gravestone of Lekoji,
son of John Anjain,
it carved "Hydrogen bomb victim #1."
A year and a week old when he became a victim,
Lekoji developed thyroid disease at fourteen
and was operated on in an American hospital.
Lekoji recovered, returned to the atoll,
entered high school, and was happy.

But soon
purple spots appeared
all over Lekoji's body,
his testicles grew swollen.
Summoned by the AEC, he changed hospitals—
Hawaii to Washington.
Semiconscious,
the count of his white blood cells falling,
he heard the sound of Rongelap waves.

Delirious, Lekoji called out:
"I want to go back to the atoll!"
"I want to eat atoll fruit!"
"I want to eat atoll fish!"
Bleeding from ears, nose, mouth,
he died
in the hospital's oxygen tent.
Nineteen years and nine months of age.
Native son of Bikini,
lifelong guinea pig of nuclear testing.

America: world's best in everything.
Atomic bomb #1,
hydrogen bomb #1,
the procession goes on, endless. . . .
Hiroshima, Nagasaki, Bikini
flow back toward America,
flow together with Nevada and Three Mile
to become a river of flames, a burning river.

—JANUARY 1980

RHM: AEC is an acronym for the Atomic Energy Commission.

MAY

The fresh new leaves on the plane trees rustle
    in the breeze,
and bright May has come to the city.
May is the season of roses,
but Kwangju's May is a sea of blood.
Blood-crazed, the army of the dictator
mauled the white bodies of the young women,
shot the students and citizens who were demonstrating,
tore fetuses from pregnant bellies
and waved them about on the points of bayonets,
split open the heads of old people, like melons.
Kwangju's May is the season of blood.

Filling the city of plane trees
with the battleship march
played at full blast,
the private armies of the fascists
swaggered through the city,
with Japanese and American flags
so large they almost dragged.
Who can say that the city through which they swaggered
won't become one day a Kwangju?
Smiling smugly, our prime minister
shakes hands with the leaders of Kwangju.
Smiling in the background:
the leader of the Western alliance.

—MAY 1980

RHM: In May 1980 the South Korean government put down a popular
uprising with great brutality. Despite Republic of Korea and U.S. claims to
the contrary, several hundred protesters died.

OUT OF THE STONE

Out of the stone they sound,
the voices of the tens of thousands who burned to death.
Charged with age-old bitter feelings,
they fill the night air.
Mul! Mul talla! Mul talla!
Water! Water, please! Water, please!

From the riverbank monument
for which there was no room in Peace Park,
all night long, they come, the voices
    of the tens of thousands dead:
Mul! Mul talla! Mul talla!

Rounded up
as they tilled the soil of Korean fields,
rounded up
as they walked the streets
of Korean towns and villages,
not allowed to say even a word of farewell
to wives and children, parents, brothers, sisters,
they were packed like livestock into transports
and shipped off, across the strait.

Forced to pray to foreign gods,
to swear allegiance to a foreign ruler,
in the end burned in that flash, they were turned
    into black corpses
for swarms of crows to peck at.

Aigu! Mul! Mul talla!
The homeland was torn in two,

and one torn half was forced to house

thousands of atomic weapons.

Why should the atom be forced

on us and our half?

Leave, you foreign soldiers!

Take your atomic bombs, and leave!

The homeland is one.

O Wind, take the message—that out of the stone

this torn half calls out to its own kind.

—JULY 1980

RHM: Hiroshima's memorial to the thousands of Koreans who died on 6 August is outside Peace Park, at the western end of one of the bridges. The strait is Tsushima Strait, which separates Korea and Japan; *aigu* is an exclamation of woe.

REFUGEES

Glossy photographs—
children in
Namibia,
Zambia,
Arabia,
Cambodia:
bellies swollen snakelike,
hands and feet feeble,
only the eyes large, hollow
and open wide,
blind from malnutrition.

You women of the north
who give your pets plenty to eat
and take them to beauty parlors,
you women and children who eat too much, don't know
    how to keep from getting fat,
and swallow reducing medicine—
the missionary from Bangladesh appealed,
"Give me some of the food
you feed your pets!"
In southern countries, eight hundred million people
    go hungry,
and forty thousand die each day of starvation.

Refugees on the ocean,
refugees in the desert,
the Israeli soldiers
who bombarded refugee tents,

the many dead like bundles of rags
lining the road.
Blood flows, a river,
and is sucked down into the dry sand.

We atomic refugees of Hiroshima—
to fill the empty stomachs of the children of
Namibia,
Zambia,
Arabia,
Cambodia,
let's change missiles into bread,
deliver
hearty human love.

—MARCH 1985

Atomic veterans of Nevada,
people living downwind from the test site—
wind that carried the ashes of death,
workers in atomic bomb factories,
operators of atomic submarines,
Bikini's atomic veterans and islanders,
those exposed to atomic power at Three Mile Island—
altogether a million people:
an atomic hell
the superpower itself has created.

At the Hiroshima gathering,
Dorothy Gangatta,
chair of the League of American Hibakusha,
bared her scars from operations for cancer of the thyroid,
cancer connected with McNamara's plans
for the production of nuclear bombs,
and appealed to us.
Among *hibakusha* of Bikini
are children who will never grow up,
mongoloids like Yuriko,
microcephalic child of Hiroshima.
In a naval hospital in Hawaii
I visited microcephalic Ike,
exposed for an instant at Bikini.
They say when Ike, now twenty-six,
sees American soldiers,
he becomes violent,
so they've put him in a mental hospital.

But Ike
smiled sweetly at us.
Atomic veterans of the United States, atomic offender,
are siblings in atomic suffering
to the *hibakusha*
of Bikini and Hiroshima-Nagasaki.

The America that already has
one million *hibakusha*
creates new *hibakusha* with each test
and is eaten away from within.
John Wayne and the whole team that filmed the Western
       on location in Nevada
died of cancer,
a strong American president
developed skin cancer on his nose
and polyps on his intestines.

Devilish weapons like SDI,
that pounces on us
with laser beams from space,
should not be permitted.
On January twenty-eighth, 1986
at the spaceport at Cape Canaveral,
at the precise moment
Americans gazed avidly into the sky,
Challenger blazed orange
and exploded,
dyeing the American sky blood-red.
As the white vapor trails vanished,
so did the members of this kamikaze space crew.

The patented spirit of Japan—
"Never give up!"—
will only make the American tragedy worse.

—FEBRUARY 1986

RHM: SDI is an acronym for Strategic Defense Initiative.

MAY IN BEIJING

—Tiananmen Square

May: season of blood and roses.
May in Kwangju.
May in Beijing.
The blood of the young flows red,
roses bloom red.

Raising the flag of nonviolence, the young people
stirred up the residents and workers,
a million people filled the square.
Voices sang the Internationale,
voices condemned to exile the old foxes, authoritarianism,
plots, ugly self-interested power,
sang, "Give us freedom!"
and the square became a people's liberated zone.
Suddenly, late at night,
a line of tanks rushes forward,
straight at the young people who occupy the square.
A roar, and shots.
Instantly the square becomes
a whirlpool of blood and screams and flames.
Red Cross ambulances
and stretchers carrying the dead and wounded.
The wild firing of crazed soldiers.
Young people fighting back, setting fire to the tanks.
On their sides and burning—hunks of metal.
The tangled long hair of blood-smeared women.
The tears on the cheeks of the young people,
glistening under the lights.

What kind of Liberation Army
runs tanks over the people when they demand liberation
and shoots them dead?
Call them what you will,
armies kill on behalf of governments.
The emperor's army that committed the massacres at Nanjing
    and in Malaysia,
the People's Liberation Army that in time of peace
surrounds its own people with tanks and massacres them:
how are they different?
China—land of Oriental generosity and decorum,
land of Lao-tzu's nonaction:
the army changed all that.

Like raging waves, voices of protest rise
all over China,
the world mourns the sons
who shed their blood for freedom
and focuses its anger on the power of the old foxes.

May: season of blood and roses.
May in Kwangju.
May in Beijing.
The blood of the young flows red,
roses bloom red.

—JUNE 1989

Presented on 6 June 1989 to a gathering, held at Memorial Hall in
Hiroshima, to express concern over events in China.

HIROSHIMA, AUSCHWITZ:
WE MUST NOT FORGET

What Auschwitz left behind:
mounds of striped inmate uniforms, children's small shoes,
and girls' red ribbons,
eating bowls that served also as chamber pots,
soap made from human fat,
cloth woven of human hair.

What Auschwitz left behind:
turn all the world's blue skies and seas into ink
and there still wouldn't be enough
    to express the sadness, the anger,
the moans of those burned in the ovens.

What Hiroshima and Nagasaki left behind:
a human shape burned onto stone,
black rain streaking a wall,
radioactivity inside bodies,
microcephalic babies irradiated in the womb,
voices of the dead sounding from the skies,
voices of the dead sounding from the bowels of the earth.

Hiroshima, Auschwitz: we must not forget.
Nagasaki, Auschwitz: we must not forget.
Even if the first time was a mistake,
the second time will be calculated malice.
The vow we made to the dead: we must not forget.

—DECEMBER 1989

RAIN

"Oh, for some rain!" had become
almost a greeting,
and now the rain falls.

It falls
on fields, hills, rivers, sea,
and concrete-jungle cities.
Carrying exhaust fumes and death ash,
the rain falls.

When the rain stops,
ultraviolet rays will pour down
out of a sky whose ozone is gone.
Living creatures will have no place to hide,
and the rays will fall.

Rain or shine, something falls.
On this latter-day world, lawless, corrupt,
the rain falls.

—JUNE 1990

RATHER THAN WEAPONS, ROSES

War: blood flows in rivers,
flows and is sucked into the sand—
futile affair.

If war starts in the desert
the desert will be red with blood,
corpses will lie exposed to the hot sun
and the stench of rotten flesh
will flow out into the whole world.

Families in the United States
will pray for the safety of loved ones,
but fathers, children, husbands, lovers
will come back in body bags—
this while families are still weeping Vietnam tears.

When the young people of the United States
come home in body bags,
America will ask that Japan, too, shed young blood,
show the rising-sun flag in the Gulf,
give money, supplies, lives.
Setting Grenada and Panama aside,
the United States confronts the Arabs:
the Palestinian problem is past, unreal,
but Kuwait is real.

Black fuselages of high-tech weapons
crisscross the Arabian sky,
black smoke billows,
sirens scream—

forty-five years ago we too
lived in and out of air-raid shelters, night and day.
Babies and the sick we took with us; fear immobilized us.
And at the end of it all,
Hiroshima was burned alive in the atomic flash.
Don't let the people of the desert
be wiped out by atomic and biochemical weapons.

Armed force won't bring peace.
Stop the blasphemous broad-daylight carnage!
Japan, first country in the world
to renounce war for reasons of conscience:
the warlike may criticize us
as unrealistic, one-country pacifists,
but let's stop them
from stuffing young people into body bags.
Don't let the rising-sun flag wave again.

Rather than weapons, roses,
rather than sanctions, talks;
no side has hands
unstained by blood.

—JANUARY 1991

THE NUCLEAR AGE

"YOU'RE NEXT!"

The atoms boil,
the atoms bubble—
gnawing at bones,
attacking blood—
day and night, the atoms boil,
night and day, the atoms bubble.

"You're next!"—
one person dies,
and someone at the wake
becomes next in line
in the atomic city into which death moved
like a hermit crab,
eyes with atomic cataracts
see only black spots
that move round and round;
the atoms boil,
the atoms bubble.

The black spots spread to cover the earth,
the atoms boil,
the atoms bubble,
a bomb explodes,
and one after the other, countless bombs explode,
the earth becomes a barren desert
like the moon,
and in the dead desert
remnant radioactivity
bubbles on.

—JUNE 1960

HIROSHIMA

I was born in the crater
of a hell that lit up the sky.
I was born in blood that flowed
in the delta's rivers, choked with blistered corpses.
I was born on a deathbed
coated with the blood of burned corpses.
I was born from the pained wish
of those breathing their last
on dirt floors of emergency morgues
stinking of blood and pus,
of victims all smeared with white salve:
"Oh, to see blue sky once more!"
I was born from the burning thirst
of people pleading in feeble voices:
"Water! Water! Please, water!"
I was born in a people-less city,
a meteorite—everything gone,
the deep stillness singing a song without words.
I was born,
and ugly clouds hung low over my future,
and in these clouds a still vaster hell
was being primed.
The flashes came:
Bikini
Sahara
Nevada
Novaya Zemlya
Takla Makan—
festivals of destruction strong enough to push the globe
        from its orbit.

Yet my tears are deeper than Bikini's sea,
my anger is stronger than Nevada's blasts,
my love is greater than Novaya Zemlya's sands.
My prayers will transform Takla Makan's desert
into fertile green fields.

—AUGUST 1960

TWENTIETH-CENTURY SAILING

—For the ship protesting
the Soviet nuclear tests

This is a twentieth-century
sailing, new,
and the prayer
of Hiroshima in ruins.
Over seas on which death ash falls,
the white-sailed *Phoenix* sets out
for the country of the dark north.

This is a twentieth-century Sermon on the Mount.
Now, down from the mountain,
Christ goes on board
and sails from the sea of Hiroshima . . .
to join hands with brethren in the country of the far north.

This is a twentieth-century ark.
It sails for the dark northern sea
to avert apocalypse.
For the sake of the *Phoenix*, disciple of peace,
storms—don't blow,
seas—don't rage.

—OCTOBER 1961

RHM: A group of American Quakers sailed the *Phoenix* from Hiroshima to
Vladivostok; one of the crew was Barbara Reynolds, a figure widely revered
in Hiroshima. She came to Hiroshima with her husband, a doctor at the
ABCC; she was a founder of the World Friendship Center in Hiroshima
and, after her return to the U.S., of the Wilmington College Peace Resource
Center (Wilmington, Ohio). On her death in 1989, Kurihara wrote a moving
tribute (typescript). *The New York Times* took no notice of the *Phoenix*.

JAPAN'S WINTER OF 1961

And now
dark winter comes to the islands of Japan;
particles the eye can't see
fall onto petals of chrysanthemums still in bloom,
onto leaves still clinging to roadside trees;
they fall
onto the soft hair of children,
onto the shoulders and backs of farm women in the fields,
soundlessly, they fall
onto city buildings,
into island rain barrels,
they fall
onto the cenotaph in Peace Park,
onto the grassy mound over the mass grave,
and the patients in the atomic hospital shake with terror.

The sea of banners that surged
under the June sun has receded,
the voices from Niijima and Miho that sang out so
have rippled away,
and onto the islands of Japan
particles the eye can't see
continue to fall.

—NOVEMBER 1961

RHM: Niijima and Miho were locations for missile sites and places of note
in the summer 1960 demonstrations against the U.S.-Japan Security Treaty.

RAVISHED CITY

In the ravished city far below,
city above which the sky once split open black,
new buildings stand in a row, like white grave markers.
Summer:
at windows
crape myrtle blossoms, like blood-soaked cotton,
and in our hearts,
undying memories of black eclipse.

Suddenly lit up by the flash, the eclipse fades
to reveal sharp outlines.
Under the split-open sky,
burned out as far as the eye can see,
a repository for blackened corpses.
Nevada and
Novaya Zemlya explode,
Bikini and
Semipalatinsk explode,
black sharks float on the ocean,
nuclear torpedoes deep in their entrails.
Moscow, Washington—
forever five seconds away from the button.

In our Hiroshima
it is still 8:15 A.M.
Amid the thunder of destruction:
the shrieks of human beings burning to death.
The dying cry of a mother holding her baby.
Naked corpses

clustered about a gangplank at the river,
scorched by the sun.

So spare us
your yammering
and your commercials!
The sky over Hiroshima is split open;
the earth is bones and rubble.
No matter what antics
you put on,
the ghosts of the dead stare, eyes fixed.

—JULY 1963

Those who brag of their power
die by their power.
January fourteenth, 1969:
the *Enterprise* goes up in flames.
A cold wind blows. Floating on the ashen sea
like a giant dead fish, the hulk remains—
U.S.A. lost to flames
flaring within.
Like meteorites on the surface of the moon,
bomb craters pit the flight deck, proud roost
        of a hundred Phantoms.
Smoke issues from below,
and skeletons of burning Phantoms
lie scattered about
like blackened grasshoppers,

Nuclear bombs filled with cities of corpses
are stored deep in the hold,
and if they exploded all at once,
the blue flash would reach
the American heartland
and expose their own evil
in a light brighter than the sun.
Sign of a great crime,
the mushroom cloud will float on the horizon.
The Hawaiian islands will be reduced to sand and blown
        away,
the sea will bubble hot,
and thousands of water columns
will rise into the sky.

The Pacific will become forever a sea of death;
Cut off by the ashes of death,
the sun over the sea
will go blind.

On January nineteenth of last year
it entered Sasebo
with a crew of 4,600,
it left port
protected by 5,000 riot police
and chased by swirling voices: *"Enterprise*—get out!"
Following the captured spy-ship *Pueblo,*
it went north into the sea of blizzards,
and turning south, sailed deep into Tonkin Gulf.
Ringleader: loosing its Phantoms,
it rained cluster bombs,
dropped napalm,
honeycombed the tender bodies
of Vietnamese women and children.

Carrying thousands of Hiroshimas and Nagasakis,
it became itself Hiroshima and Nagasaki,
U.S.A.—country that will perish by fire.
On the eve of that fire,
the *Enterprise* goes up in flames.

—JANUARY 1969

RHM: Sasebo is a port and U.S. naval base on the west coast of Kyushu near Nagasaki. For press coverage of the incident, see the *New York Times,* 15 January 1969 and the following days. Kurihara reissued the poem in June 1990 when the carrier *Midway* was rocked by explosions. In a note she stated: "Even in today's era of nuclear arms reductions, the concern with nukes remains as always—in that, there isn't the slightest change."

On the riverbanks
in the park,
cherry blossoms bloom like cotton candy,
and people climb down from tourist buses
to face the tombstone that swells like the back
     of a dead horse
and snap their snapshots.
She poses
with the abstract monument
as backdrop—
and doesn't the blue light suddenly flash?
The monument's mother, babe, and small daughters—
aren't they blown to smithereens?
The cherries in full blossom like cotton candy—
don't they turn to flame, swirl inside the park,
and, crossing the river,
collide with flames on the other side?
Doesn't the river flow straight up into the sky,
become a cyclone,
and take people and trees and buildings
high up into the air?

The naked dead who crowded together that day
on the granite slopes of the riverbank
sank into the cold river,
and in the eyes of the dead
the cherries blossoming palely like cotton candy
still appear the color of flame.
This year, too, the cherry trees in the park
intertwine their branches, and the road along the river

is a bright arcade of flowers.

But this season in Japan

is a season of bitter demonstrations—

young people, eyes overflowing from the shroud

of tear gas, throwing rocks.

It is a season of the blood of young people

with broken skulls.

It is a season of flames

when the cherry trees inside the barricades

suddenly blaze up.

—JULY 1969

RHM: The abstract monument is not the cenotaph but a sculpture by
Hongō Shin (1905–80). Titled "Mother and Children in the Tempest" (1953),
it is situated on the southern edge of Peace Park.

The world sinks toward evening;
in the ashen sky
shades drift, drift in the wind.
Dawn, dawn:
it will not come again.

Flowers
trees
butterflies
birds
cats
dogs
human beings:
all living things, not to be born again,
become mere shades
trembling like ribbons,
shrinking like balloons,
bursting like bubbles.
Without a word of resentment
they drift, drift in the wind.
Dawn: it will not come again.
Dawn: it will not come again.

—OCTOBER 1971

CONCENTRIC CIRCLES

—Iwakuni, Hiroshima

A strip of meadow,
covered with dry, rustling reeds,
and rising rooflike out of the ground:
six silos.
It is not New Mexico's
Los Alamos.
Iwakuni: thirty miles from Hiroshima,
outside the concentric circles of death
August sixth.
Iwakuni: strategic Far Eastern base,
swollen by the withdrawal from Vietnam.
Poison gas and CBW units
are stationed here,
and Skyhawks with atomic payloads
take off, land.

Behind concrete walls
tens of yards thick
they are stored, those spindle-shaped objects.
They dream
of the day they'll be triggered
to create the landscape of doomsday.
The meadow's
off-limits to Japanese,
and in the landscape of death that surrounds it,
evil black birds already circle
in search of corpses. . . .
Suddenly, above the band of protesters,
Phantoms wheel,

tearing open the late autumn sky—
scheduled death flights
linking Iwakuni, Okinawa, Vietnam.

With a thin smile,
the local Self-Defense Agency man says,
"No comment."
The base commander says,
"The President has jurisdiction,
so no comment."
The mayor of Iwakuni says,
"The town has no authority to investigate,
so no comment."
In the Diet the violent majority
rams decisions through and slaps the people down—
Japan: one-time ally of the Nazis.
Japan: current ally of atomic imperialism.

Exposed to the chill wind,
hibakusha now grown old
put anemic lives on the line
and hold a sit-in in front of the gates.
Though they've kept on shouting ever since that day,
though they've kept on calling out ever since that day,
they've been shoved all the way inside
the concentric circles of death.
Iwakuni, Hiroshima.

And yet
the atomic curse must be broken.
The concentric circles of death
must be turned into concentric circles of peace.
—Because it is our wish, we who survived that day

yet could only watch helplessly
as the others were burned alive.
—Because it is the wish
of all living creatures.

—NOVEMBER 1971

RHM: CBW is an acronym for "chemical and biological weapons." The
"violent majority" is the Liberal Democratic Party.

Suddenly
the blue flash lit up the sky,
and under the cloud
of the swirling firestorm
black uranium rain fell,
and in the burning fires
young and old burned to death.
Survivors dragged broken hearts and broken bodies
into the dark cave
of atomic autism
and even dreamed of demonic equity:
"Wouldn't it be fine if bombs fell—
thump! thump!—all over the world.
Then people might understand
the suffering the atomic bomb brings."

The flash burned out the city,
blew away buildings,
filled the seven rivers with corpses,
scorched the very souls of those who survived.
But it didn't destroy discrimination.
Buraku hibakusha, excluded,
and Korean *hibakusha* with nowhere to go
built shacks of burned tin
in segregated *buraku*
on the banks of rivers
that burned with remnant radioactivity
and have lived bloodied
     by the thorns of discrimination.
"*Hibakusha* blood won't clot."

"It's genetic."
"Don't marry your daughter to one. Don't marry one."
Dark whispers
are still exchanged,
and the bonds of the spell become several times heavier.

Why was the bomb dropped?
Let *hibakusha* crawl out
of the cave of atomic autism,
and proclaim to the world
their *hibakusha*-hood:
"Don't create more *hibakusha*!"
Why were there Korean victims?
Mothers threw away the *urimaru*
and acted like *uenamu*—let them put a stop to all that
and issue a proclamation of their Korean-hood.
Why are there *buraku*?
Let them stop living in hiding
like underground Christians
and proclaim their *buraku*-hood.
Let those robbed of their humanity
rise up
and denounce the source of oppression.
The future begins here.

Amid the rubble that covered the Parade Ground
stood an iron bed from the army hospital,
burned bright red.
On the bed, like fish on a grill,
a row
of human bodies—
white bones only.
Along with Auschwitz,

Hiroshima

is the world's darkest abyss.
It is a city of atrocity
where those who were robbed of their humanity
live like pale shades.
Humans turned into shades: let's rise up
and bring to an end the age of the mushroom cloud
that mocks humanity.

Skin color may differ,
but in the hell beneath the mushroom cloud
yellow, black, white are all the same.
The slowly shuffling group going nowhere
under a sky
in which the firestorm roars,
skin torn off and protruding,
hanging off in ribbons,
hands dangling like ghosts.
Piles of naked corpses swollen
and burned to the core, charred black.
Before the globe burns
and flowers don't bloom and birds don't sing
and the uranium cloud
hangs low
and helium rain pours down
and the globe becomes a dead planet,
let's restore the humanity stolen from us.
If humans don't drop the bomb, it won't fall.
There is nothing humans have made
that human hands cannot stop.

—FEBRUARY 1977

RHM: *Buraku* (or *burakumin*) are outcasts. The literal meaning of the term is
"village." *Urimaru* is Korean for "mother tongue"; *uenamu* is Korean for
"Japanese."

HIROSHIMA, NAGASAKI, HARRISBURG AFLAME

In the beginning was a uranium hell.
In the beginning was a plutonium hell.

A blue flash lighting up the sky.
An orange fireball
enveloping the earth.
Directly underneath: a five-hundred-meter circle turned
        into a sea of fire
permeated by eight thousand rads of radiation.

People, trees, even flowers
were burned black, evaporated, blown away by the firestorm.
The radioactivity that spread out in concentric circles
still burns away inside people today,
and one day, suddenly, they fall ill.

After the war ended,
a reborn Hiroshima was packaged in rosy colors
and became a myth of the atomic age
transmitted to the whole world.
Nuclear-power-plant seacoast where, suddenly,
spiderwort mutates.
Trace radiation spewing out of drainpipes.
Trace radiation in warm coolant
discharging into the ocean.
Million-kilowatt reactors
a thousand Hiroshimas strong
dreaming of sudden explosion.

March twenty-eighth, 1979, before dawn:
in the control room
of Reactor #2 on the Susquehanna
the computer kept showing a question mark.
Bubbling in the reactor's core, coolant escaped,
and the chamber became a pool of boiling water.
The ECCS didn't work,
the zirconium of the fuel rods began to melt,
and the core generated hydrogen.
Gamma rays passed through steel walls
five inches thick,
broke through thick concrete walls.

On the third day
they ordered pregnant women and children to leave
and completed a paper plan for evacuation,
a twenty-two-mile radius, 636,000 people.
Contaminated by radiation,
people, cats, dogs vomited,
buds on roadside trees, just out,
turned black and withered.
Middletown became a ghost town,
in Harrisburg, twelve miles away,
panic set in city-wide.
Blowing in the wind,
radioactive gas
rose into the clouds and drifted
to New York, to Canada.
For the next twenty years, those within an eighteen-mile
        radius
will get medical check-ups
and have nightmares of Hiroshima.

In the beginning was a uranium hell.
In the beginning was a plutonium hell.
Once the war ended,
the nuclear powers and the merchants of death
sealed Hiroshima off—a peace capsule—
and with banknotes and nightsticks kept the lid on.
Hiroshima, Nagasaki, Harrisburg—
nuclear sister-cities.
Turning the jets of radioactive flame back at those
        who launch them,
we race around the globe, arm in arm,
appearing at struggles all over the world
to denounce the hell of radioactivity.

—APRIL 1979

RHM: ECCS is an acronym for Emergency Core-Cooling System.

THE OTHER CLOCK

Red cyclamens are blooming in windows,
and New Year's has come,
but the other clock stands
at three minutes to zero hour.

Is there nothing mothers can do
but kiss their children goodbye
and wait for the end?
In Europe Pershing IIs
have already been shipped in,
in the Western Pacific Tomahawks will be deployed in June.
With each moment that passes, zero hour draws nearer.

So that their children's future will not be erased,
so that radioactive dust will not block out the sun
and turn the globe into a cold, dark ruin,
the women of Europe
formed a human chain around the military base.

Let the sun shine down on the children.
Let the children chase butterflies, dragonflies, cicadas
in field and forest.

Three minutes to zero hour:
the women of Japan must act!

—JANUARY 1983

Zero hour is the end brought about by nuclear war.

RHM: The military base is Greenham Common, a U.S. base in Great Britain
and the site throughout the 1980s of an extended protest by British women
against the introduction of cruise missiles.

LET THE SUN SHINE ON THE CHILDREN

After the nuclear-powered carrier *Carl Vinson*
dropped anchor in Tokyo Bay, near Japan's capital,
the fortieth New Year's turned heavy and harsh.
The New Year we welcomed amid the atomic ruins
was a cold New Year: no rice cakes, no festive foods,
powdery snow dancing in
through cracks in makeshift huts.
Still, families nodded in approval:
the sky
held no more blue flashes,
firebombs no longer fell.

But the dead did not come back,
and the survivors vomited blood
and died of atomic sickness.
Mistreated because of fears that atomic sickness
        was contagious,
living in farm sheds and makeshift huts,
people even dreamed of a satanic impartiality:
"Would that atomic bombs went off with a bang
the world over!"

In Year Ten, as they tested the H-bomb at Bikini,
people finally stirred, joined hands,
        and said between sobs: "Glad we survived!"
In Year Thirty-five,
taken to task with the words,
        "All Japanese must persevere,"
aged *hibakusha* trembled with rage.
Living forgotten lives

in odd corners of a booming city,
second and third generations suddenly
        were dying of leukemia,
microcephalics were babbling baby talk.

In Year Forty they extended the atomic barb
even out into space,
and the doomsday clock stood at three minutes to midnight.
There will be no broadcast bulletins of war's outbreak,
but one day, suddenly, the sky will flash blue,
radioactive dust will hide the sun,
and earth will enter the cold dark of nuclear winter.

Even if the first time was a mistake,
the second time will be treachery.
Let us not forget our pledge to the dead.
Stop the clock before it's too late.
Let the sun shine on the children.
Let's bring back the lost smell of plants
        and the voices of song,
lift up our eyes, and stride toward tomorrow.

—JANUARY 1985

Nineteen thirty-three:
the strongest Eastern power, isolated,
withdrew from the League of Nations.
Forty-two against one boded disaster.
Nineteen forty:
three despots formed an alliance.
Poets sang the praises
of *Hinomaru* and *Hakenkreuz*.

Waving small *Hinomarus*,
women sent husbands, sons, lovers off to war.
And went home to weep secret tears.
"Give birth!" "Multiply!"—to increase "human resources,"
women were made into child-bearing machines;
if you bore ten children, you received a decoration—
    "Patriotic Mother."
Women surrendered pots and kettles,
gongs and candlesticks from the *butsudan*,
even wedding rings, to be made into weapons.
They couldn't give their children even single toffees—
"Covet nothing till victory is ours"—
had to feed them ersatz foods—soy waste fit only for pigs—
    and locusts,
bitter dumplings made with horseweed,
and let them be led to believe in the Divine Wind.
Each day they chanted,
"We were born for the Emperor,
and we'll die happily for the Emperor."
Attached to all orders were the tired words,
"His August Majesty graciously . . . ,"

and women could only stand at attention and obey.
Mobilized to work in munitions plants,

they had to work, dizzy from malnutrition,

right up to menopause.

August sixth, 1945:

in Hiroshima nearly nine thousand schoolchildren,

mobilized for the fourth clearing of firebreaks

were roasted to death in the hot rays.

Pursued by the firestorm that raged and roared,

they jumped into the rivers with their teachers,

they sang the anthem

      and shouted *banzai* for the emperor,

called out "Mother!" and drowned.

Banzai for the emperor—words

their teachers taught them;

"Mother!"—a cry from their very souls.

In 1985, the fortieth year after the war ended,

we are rich in material goods, our desires have grown large,

and we've forgotten all about starvation

and the taste of bitter dumplings

Children starving in Africa:

something happening far away.

Tomahawks are brought into port,

joint U.S.-Japanese military exercises are held—

"the Russians will land in Hokkaido"—

tanks are brought from Korea

to the U.S. Army's supply depot in Sagamihara,

the roar of tanks becomes oppressive.

The world is about to enter

the dark and cold of nuclear winter.

yet our faces remain blank, we middle-class clones.

We—we won't repeat the mistake?

Japanese teachers won't ever send their pupils off to war?

Let's answer the children

who with their last breaths cried out, "Mother!"

Let all women join hands

and prevent all the babies on earth

from being burned to death.

Let's turn male principles—bullets and bombs—

into female principles—life and peace.

With hope for the new year. . . .

—APRIL 1985

RHM: The *Hinomaru* is the Japanese flag (rising sun); *Hakenkreuz* is the swastika. On "human resources," see also "Respect for Humanity" above. The Divine Wind (*kamikaze*) is the superhuman agency protecting Japan, as against the Mongol fleets in the late thirteenth century.

Alphabetical List of Poems by Title in English